# Lecture Notes of the Institute for Computer Sciences, Social Informatics and Telecommunications Engineering 665

The LNICST series publishes ICST's conferences, symposia and workshops.

LNICST reports state-of-the-art results in areas related to the scope of the Institute.

The type of material published includes

- Proceedings (published in time for the respective event)
- Other edited monographs (such as project reports or invited volumes)

LNICST topics span the following areas:

- General Computer Science
- E-Economy
- E-Medicine
- Knowledge Management
- Multimedia
- Operations, Management and Policy
- Social Informatics
- Systems

Raghvendra Kumar · Priyadarsan Parida ·
Prasant Kumar Pattnaik
Editors

# Next Generation Computing and Communication Applications

First EAI International Conference, ICNGCCA 2025
Odisha, India, March 18, 2025
Proceedings

Springer

*Editors*
Raghvendra Kumar
GIET University
Gunupur, Odisha, India

Priyadarsan Parida
GIET University
Gunupur, Odisha, India

Prasant Kumar Pattnaik
KIIT University
Bhubaneswar, Odisha, India

ISSN 1867-8211 ISSN 1867-822X (electronic)
Lecture Notes of the Institute for Computer Sciences, Social Informatics and Telecommunications Engineering
ISBN 978-3-032-13008-2 ISBN 978-3-032-13009-9 (eBook)
https://doi.org/10.1007/978-3-032-13009-9



This Springer imprint is published by the registered company Springer Nature Switzerland AG
The registered company address is: Gewerbestrasse 11, 6330 Cham, Switzerland

# Preface

We are pleased to present the proceedings of the European Alliance for Innovation (EAI) 1st International Conference on Next Generation Computing and Communication Applications (EAI ICNGCCA 2025). Hosted by GIET University, Gunupur, India, the conference was held on March 18, 2025. This conference successfully brought together researchers, developers, and practitioners from around the globe who are advancing and leveraging smart grid technologies to create smarter, more resilient systems. The theme of EAI ICNGCCA 2025, "Next Generation Computing and Communication with Emerging Technologies", set the stage for an engaging and insightful program.

The technical agenda featured 10 full papers across two main conference tracks: Track 1: Foundational Models of Machine Learning and Big Data and Track 2: Emerging Trends for Big Data Analytics for Next Generation Computing, We were honored to host two keynote speeches by distinguished experts: Manju Khari (Jawaharlal Nehru University, India) on "Ethical Guidelines for AI in Healthcare" and Noor Zaman Jhanjhi (Taylor's University, Malaysia) on "Autonomous Systems: From Self-Driving Cars to Intelligent Robotics". These papers were selected from 122 submissions. Each submission was reviewed following a double-blind process with a minimum of 3 reviews per paper.

The success of the conference was made possible through the exceptional coordination with our Steering Chairs, K. Murali Gopal and Bibhu Prasad of GIET University, Gunupur, India. We sincerely appreciate their unwavering support and guidance. It was also a privilege to collaborate with an outstanding organizing committee, whose dedication ensured the smooth execution of the event. Special thanks are due to the Technical Program Committee, led by our TPC Co-Chairs Vassilis C. Gerogiannis (University of Thessaly, Greece), Ajit Kumar Patro (GIET University, India), and Nilamdhab Padhy (GIET University, India) for their diligent peer-review efforts, resulting in a high-quality technical program. We are also grateful to Conference Manager Patrícia Gabajová for her invaluable support, and to all the authors who submitted their work to EAI ICNGCCA 2025. We firmly believe that EAI ICNGCCA 2025 provided a vibrant forum for researchers, developers, and practitioners to explore and discuss scientific and technological advancements relevant to the future of smart grids. We are confident that future editions of the conference will continue to be as successful and inspiring as reflected by the outstanding contributions compiled in this volume.

Raghvendra Kumar
Priyadarsan Parida
Prasant Kumar Pattnaik

# Organization

## Steering Committee

| | |
|---|---|
| Satya Prakash Panda | GIET University, India |
| Chandra Dhwaj Panda | GIET University, India |
| Jagadish Panda | GIET University, India |
| A. V. N. L. Sharma | GIET University, India |
| N. V. Jagannadha Rao | GIET University, India |

## Organizing Committee

### General Chairs

| | |
|---|---|
| Prasant Kumar Pattnaik | KIIT University, India |
| Lalit Mohan Patnaik | GIET University, India |
| Tanupriya Choudhury | University of Petroleum and Energy Studies, India |

### General Co-chairs

| | |
|---|---|
| Le Hoang Son | Vietnam National University, Vietnam |
| Bibhu Prasad | GIET University, India |
| K. Murali Gopal | GIET University, India |

### Program Co-chairs

| | |
|---|---|
| Raghvendra Kumar | GIET University, India |
| Ankit Vishnoi | Symbiosis International, India |
| Priyadarsan Parida | GIET University, India |
| Jung Sup Um | Kyungpook National University, South Korea |

### TPC Co-chairs

| | |
|---|---|
| Noor Zaman Jhanjhi | Taylor's University, Malaysia |
| Vassilis C. Gerogiannis | University of Thessaly, Greece |
| Ajit Kumar Patro | GIET University, India |
| Nilamdhab Padhy | GIET University, India |

### Sponsorship and Exhibit Chairs

| | |
|---|---|
| Sachikanta Dash | GIET University, India |
| Jitendra Kumar | GIET University, India |

### Local Chairs

| | |
|---|---|
| Padmini Mishra | GIET University, India |
| S. N. Das | GIET University, India |
| Richa Chaudhary | UPES Dehradun, India |
| Tridha Bajaja | UPES Dehradun, India |
| Rasmita Panigrahi | GIET University, India |
| Bandana Mallick | GIET University, India |

### Workshops Chairs

| | |
|---|---|
| A. V. S. Pavan Kumar | GIET University, India |
| Manoj Kumar Panda | Petronas, Malaysia |
| Sandeep Chandola | UPES Dehradun, India |
| Sudeshna Chakraborty | Galgotias University, India |

## Publicity and Social Media Chairs

| | |
|---|---|
| Hussain Falih Mahdi | University of Diyala, Iraq |
| Ribhu Abhusan Panda | GIET University, India |
| Nilamdhab Padhy | GIET University, India |
| K. Siva Krishna | GIET University, India |

## Publications Chairs

| | |
|---|---|
| Nilambar Sethi | GIET University, India |
| Tusar Kanta Panda | GIET University, India |
| Jung Sup Um | Kyungpook National University, South Korea |
| Vaclav Skala | University of West Bohemia, Czech Republic |
| Ankur Dixit | Cornell University, USA |

## Web Chairs

| | |
|---|---|
| Bidush Kumar Sahoo | GIET University, India |
| Ranjita Rout | GIET University, India |

## Posters and PhD Track Chairs

| | |
|---|---|
| Sibo Prasad Patro | GIET University, India |
| Ashima Sindhu Mohanty | GIET University, India |
| B. J. Kim | Sookmyung Women's University, South Korea |
| Dhiraj Kumar | AT&S, Austria |

## Panels Chairs

| | |
|---|---|
| Premansusekhara Rath | GIET University, India |
| Radhanath Patra | GIET University, India |
| Harshit Bhatia | IFP Energies Nouvelles, France |
| Richa Chaudhry | UPES Dehradun, India |
| Roohi Sille | UPES Dehradun, India |
| Shahina Anwarul | UPES Dehradun, India |
| Avita Katal | Galgotias University, India |

## Demos Chairs

| | |
|---|---|
| Ami Kumar Parida | GIET University, India |
| B. B. Biswal | GIET University, India |
| Subarna Shakya | Tribhuvan University, Nepal |

## Tutorials Chairs

| | |
|---|---|
| Jyotirmaya Mishra | GIET University, India |
| Ashish Tiwary | GIET University, India |
| Thinagaran Perumal | Universiti Putra Malaysia, Malaysia |
| Hiral Desai | Vanguard Dallas, USA |

## Technical Program Committee

| | |
|---|---|
| Akshay Kumar Swain | University of Auckland, New Zealand |
| Alekha Mishra | NIT Jamshedpur, India |
| Alok Tripathy | Ravenshaw University, India |
| Anitha A. | Vellore Institute of Technology, India |
| Bibudhendu Pati | Rama Devi Women's University (Govt.), India |
| Debendra Ku Das | University of Alaska, USA |
| Deepak Tosh | University of Texas at El Paso, USA |
| Gopal Behera | Government College of Engineering Kalahandi, India |
| Lalitha Krishnasamy | CHRIST (Deemed to be University), India |
| Manoj Kumar | University of Wollongong in Dubai, UAE |
| Praveen Kumar | Innopolis University, Russia |
| Punyaban Patel | C.M.R. College of Engineering & Technology, India |
| Purna Sethi | Rama Devi Women's University, India |
| Raghunandan Swain | Parala Maharaja Engineering College, India |
| S. Gopal Krishna Patro | GIET University, India |
| Sangita Pal | IGIT Sarang, India |
| Sasmita Acharya | VSSUT, India |
| Satyasundara Mahapatra | Pranveer Singh Institute of Technology, India |
| Shinya Inazumi | Shibaura Institute of Technology, Japan |
| Srinivas Sethi | IGIT Sarang, India |
| Suman Das | University of Brescia, Italy |
| Vaclav Skala | University of West Bohemia/University of Defence, Czech Republic |

# Contents

# Machine Learning

# Optimizing Ad Campaigns: A Deep Dive into Machine Learning Strategies for Advertising Agencies

Vivek Kumar Prasad[1], Debabrata Dansana[2](✉), D. Anil Kumar[3], Santosh Kumar Panda[3], and Tanmaya Bhoi[2]

[1] Nirma University, Gujarat, Ahmedabad, India
[2] Rajendra University, Balangir, Odisha, India
debabratadansana07@gmail.com
[3] GIET University, Gunupur, Odisha, India

**Abstract.** Since their creation, machine learning and artificial intelligence have become a part of our daily lives. A branch of artificial intelligence known as "machine learning" is a flexible concept with applications in nearly every field, including agriculture, industry, and medicine. One significant use of machine learning is targeted advertising, a strategy nearly all businesses use to increase sales. Advertising is essential for a company's brand value, and the current trend shows that almost everything is done online, where tailored advertising comes into play. Targeted advertising is highly profitable, with companies like Google and Facebook generating significant revenue by targeting users and promoting their clients' products. Users are served advertisements based on their past ac tivities and interests, increasing the likelihood and success rate of purchases. Machine learning facilitates this by creating models that calculate the probability of a customer clicking on an advertisement. Decision trees and logistic regression are two effective methods for predicting this probability accurately. In this paper, we highlight how these methods identify the correct target audience and determine how likely they are to engage with the advertised product.

**Keywords:** Machine Learning · Decision Trees · Targeted Advertising · Logistic Regression · Neural Networks · Fuzzy Model · Cross-Validation Method · Confu- sion Matrix

## 1 Introduction

Data mining now uses direct marketing as a key application area. In this, businesses and organizations contact their clients directly and target them specifically for sales or fundraising. Large databases are kept up to support this. Databases assist in choosing the target clients by providing various details, such as personal information (age, history, gender) [1]. A crucial data mining issue within direct advertising is target selection. The primary goal of Target Selection is to find possible clients for a commodity from a


R. Kumar et al. (Eds.): ICNGCCA 2025, LNICST 665, pp. 3–14, 2026.
https://doi.org/10.1007/978-3-032-13009-9_1

customer database by identifying the profiles of persons who have previously expressed interest in the product. Several methods can be used, including fuzzy clustering, neural computing, statistical regression, and decision trees (CART/CHAID) [2]. This study will use cross-validation (mean and standard deviation) to distinguish. Between various target advertising techniques [3]. Target advertising ideas will be discussed at the beginning of this paper, followed by several strategies, their uses, cross-validation techniques, a comparison of the models' performances, and a conclusion [4, 5].

## 2 Literature Survey

The optimization of advertising campaigns through the integration of machine learning strategies has become pivotal in enhancing the efficacy of digital marketing efforts. The author provided a comprehensive review outlining the applications of machine learning in online advertising, emphasizing its influence on targeting, personalization, and overall campaign optimization. As explored by the author, adaptive machine learning models offer the ability to dynamically adjust to evolving user behaviors and market trends, ensuring campaigns remain responsive to changing conditions [6]. Additionally, as investigated by the author [7], deploying deep learning approaches holds promise in further refining ad campaign optimization, particularly using neural networks. Reinforcement learning's role in advertising was surveyed and highlighted for its potential to optimize campaigns by learning from user interactions [8]. A comparative analysis of machine learning algorithms for ad campaign optimization by the author offers insights into different algorithms' relative strengths and weaknesses [9]. Exploration of predictive analytics in advertising underscores machine learning's significance in predicting user behavior and tailoring ad content [10]. As discussed in [11], natural language processing techniques enhance customer engagement by analyzing and understanding textual data in ad campaigns. The author light on machine learning-based personalization, emphasizing the ability to tailor ad content to individual user preferences [12]. While the specific papers are not available in the referenced literature, these studies collectively highlight the diverse and impactful role of machine learning in optimizing advertising campaigns. [13–16].

The rest of the research work is organized in Sect. 3, where material and methods are discussed; in Sect. 4, proposed targeted advertising techniques and methodology are discussed; in Sect. 5, implementations and results; and the re- search work is concluded in Sect. 6.

## 3 Material and Methods

### 3.1 Target Selection: Basic Principles

In direct marketing, target choice is crucial. The basic task of choosing a target is to select potential buyers for an item from a database by identifying those who have previously expressed interest in it. The two methods are scoring and segmentation. Target selection based on segmentation divides clients into groups according to how well they match specific criteria. Based on training data, an estimation of the response percentage for each category can be made. Customers from the category with the greatest response percentage are chosen for a tailored offer.

Using scoring-based target selection, customers are targeted individually based on their scores. The score indicates the customer's probability of responding. The target model then forecasts each customer's response likelihood, placing orders acordingly. Only the product offer is provided to customers with a strong probability of purchasing.

### 3.2 Statistical Regression

Mathematical equations are used in statistical models to encode details obtained from data. They demonstrate simple models that assume straightforward correlations between the data, and in some cases, they generate accurate models quickly. Regression in its most popular form is linear regression. Using a variety of input variables, the models try to identify a straight line that reduces the discrepancies between the output values expected and those obtained. In this context, the training data is visualized geometrically. Each variable in the training example helps to pin- point a specific location in space. The regression equation represents a line that minimizes the average distance between these points. This line is also a predictive model when the dependent variable is known. Regression relies on input or independent variables to forecast output variables, also known as dependent or target variables.

*Logistic regression* is a more complex form of regression, yet it employs a methodology similar to linear regression. It uses a target notion with discrete values to categorize data based on input factors.

### 3.3 Decision Trees

Advertising has become increasingly audience-driven, given the inclusion of various techniques. Targeted advertising is based on keyword matching. We look for a phrase or keyword in the advertisement that lures the customer the most. Based on that, we use several supervised machine learning methods such as Logistic Regression, Support Vector Machine (SVM), Decision trees, Neural networks, etc., to determine how probable the user is to click on those ads or, in other words, what is the success rate of that advertising.

As this is a supervised learning technique, we would need to fetch the training data of multiple features. The primary source is the user's past searches regarding similar topics on the company's site or some other. The information report generated by the cookies on the company's site maintains a unique ID for each customer and the site's name. They enable the website to retrieve this information as we revisit it and tailor the page accordingly for the user.

Now, the dataset captured would consist of several features, such as time spent on the website, age, income, clicked-on ad, gender, location, etc. Each of these features plays an important role in the decision tree classification. We train our model with this data and develop an algorithm to estimate the likelihood of the user clicking on the data. The main focus of this approach is whether the user clicks on the ad or not. Since we only have two output categories, we can use two classes(yes/no) as our output labels for classifying various data.

We can use decision trees to accurately classify our data into these two categories. Decision trees are a decision support algorithm with many applications, including marketing, finance, risk prediction, medical sciences, astronomy, and production planning. Decision support is a type of Predictive Analytics method used in Machine Learning.

**How Would Decision Trees Work?**

Firstly, we must select attributes/attributes from our dataset, which will split the data based on certain parameters. These parameters vary according to the type of tree we use to decide the splitting attribute, information gain in Iterative Dichotomiser 3 (ID3), Gini index in CART, and so on. Usually, the attribute with the highest purity is selected first. There are three steps to applying decision trees to the marketing field. First, as discussed above, we would create an initial tree from our training set using attribute selection measures such as the Gini Index, Gain Ratio, and Information Gain. After that, we will try to remove those branches that do not have enough statistical data to reduce the chances of misclassification. Finally, this tree is processed to improve its understandability and generalization ability.

A decision tree has an edge because it considers many variables or features to predict the outcome. The greater the number of attributes, the lesser the chance of misclassification. Feature selection is also an important part of the decision tree algorithm. Those subsets of features that give the highest accuracy of classification are selected.

So, this gives an overview of how decision trees may be used for targeted advertising.

### 3.4 Neural Networks

Deep learning techniques are based on neural networks, a branch of machine learning. A neural network has several hidden layers and tries to replicate how the human brain functions. You may think of the hidden layers as abstract input data representations. These layers can be used to comprehend various aspects of data. We can understand the network logic using an output layer, which is considered a translator. Nodes are the basic processing elements.

Each node possesses an activity level indicating the neuron's polarization state, an output value reflecting its firing rate, sets of input and output connections, and a bias value determining the neuron's internal resting level. Real numbers mathematically represent these characteristics.

Neurons are used to process the data. Neurons that are connected employ connection links to communicate with one another by sending signals or information. The quality of these connection links determines the method of information processing. The neural network's two primary characteristics are architecture and learning.

The processing units are arranged in layers. A neural network typically comprises three main components: the input variables, represented by the input layer; one or more hidden layers; and the output variables, represented by an output layer. Each connection has a specific weight that defines how the incoming information will affect the unit's activation level. The weights might either be positive or negative. The following relationship is used for the neuron output signal:

$$\sigma = (\omega^T \chi) = (\sum^{n} \omega_j \chi_j) \tag{1}$$

where $\omega = (\omega_1, \ldots, \omega_n)^T \in R^n$ is scaled vector and $x = (x_1, \ldots, x_n)^T \in R^n$ is the neuron input vector. It's common to refer to the function $f(\omega^T x)$ as an activation func- tion. The two primary categories of activation functions are kernel functions and projection functions. Both radial basis networks and multilayer perceptrons with sigmoidal transfer functions have the theoretical capability to estimate any continu- ous function with arbitrary precision, classifying them as universal approximators. However, this does not mean identifying the optimal network to replicate a specific function can be achieved quickly or within a predetermined time frame.

Setting up the inputs in a neural network's training process ensures it can most accurately mimic the underlying function or anticipate the target concept. Under this description, training a neural network becomes an optimization problem.

Most software programs facilitate the development of neural network models that employ various backpropagation learning algorithms. Since the initial optimization method called steepest descent, used by error backpropagation networks, proved ineffective, networks using different learning algorithms, like Newton techniques, Levenberg-Marquardt, or conjugate gradients, have taken their place.

## 3.5 Fuzzy Modelling

In several fields, like control engineering, decision-making, and data mining, fuzzy models are becoming increasingly common. One of the key characteristics of fuzzy models is the way they integrate mathematical efficiency with linguistic rules, which provides transparency. Thus, fuzzy models are between numerical and symbolic models at an intermediate place. Fuzzy clustering is a widely used technique for creating fuzzy models. It involves dividing a data set into overlapping groups based on the similarity within the groups and dissimilarity between them. These algo- rithms are unsupervised methods.

Allow N data objects to contain the set $\{x1, xN\}$ where $xk \in R^n$. The object's set's data matrix X will be $N\ x\ n$ in size. The fuzzy clustering techniques compute $N$ x $C$ partition matrix U and the C-tuple of related cluster prototypes $V = \{v1, \ldots, vC\}$ to. find a fuzzy partition of X into C clusters. Data item $xk$'s membership in cluster $i$ is represented by the elements $uik \in [0, 1]$ of U.

With fuzzy c-means and the Gustafson-Kessel algorithm, the cluster prototypes are frequently points in the cluster space, i.e., $vi \in R^n$. The Gustafson-Kessel (GK) method includes an adaptive measure to adapt the clusters' structure to the data points' distribution. It leads with ellipsoidal clusters, whereas spherically distributed clusters are searched by the Fuzzy c-means algorithm within the data. Cluster prototypes are allowed by the extended Gustafson-Kessel (E-GK) and extended fuzzy c- means (E-FCM) methods in the clustering space to be closed volumes.

The number of clusters within which the data should be separated is a crucial parameter to choose in fuzzy clustering algorithms. Since it reflects a trade-off between having enough data points with high cluster membership and obtaining strong predictive models, this value must be carefully chosen for each fuzzy model.

Several approaches to target selection have been investigated using fuzzy modeling techniques based on fuzzy clustering. Takagi-Sugeno fuzzy models' optimization has turned out to be the most effective of those that use a genetic algorithm. The data were clustered using the Gustafson-Kessel clustering technique.

### 3.6 Cross-Validation of Models Using Comparison Measures

Identifying target selection models to compare the models is the first step in apply- ing the cross-validation technique. To compare the various fuzzy identification strat- egies, we shall discuss the standard deviation and mean of a certain number of models *M* in this section.

Allow N data objects to contain the set {x1, x*N*} where x*k* € $R^n$. The object's set's data matrix X will be *N x n* in size. Additionally, the data set X will be divided into *M* equal sections. Once identified, *M* models are cross-validated using these *M* partial data sets. Hit probability charts can be generated for these models; thus, the mean and standard deviation can be calculated. We can see how these models differ from one another by looking at the graph that is produced.

This is how the cross-validation will proceed:

1. Let's randomly split the set of data X into *M* equal portions, X1 to X*M*.
2. Train a model utilizing X\X*k* for $k = 1$ to *M*. Using X*k*, create a hit probability chart (*hpck*).
3. Using the assumption that all *heck* has an equal chance of occurring (i.e., 100/*M*%), get the mean of *HPC* as,
4. Determine the HPC's standard deviation as follows:

The HPC represents the average accuracy anticipated while training a model with the entire data set X.

The standard deviation of HPC indicates the level of inaccuracy in trained models on X. By utilizing the mean and standard deviation of the hit probability charts, dif- ferent models (or methods) can be compared. These metrics highlight the extent of differences between the models.

## 4 Proposed Targeted Advertising Techniques and Methodology

We will implement targeted advertising using decision trees and logistic regression instead of all the proposed methods: decision trees, support vector machine (SVM), and logistic regression. The aim is to analyze the accuracy of both approaches for predicting a common question, which is whether the user will click on the ad or not.

Imagine we work for a marketing firm. Consider this: The marketing firm must an- alyze the advertising data gathered to ascertain whether a specific user will click on the advertisement displayed to them. This can be accomplished by utilizing the right machine-learning method. Thus, we could generalize our model for a broader sample area, which would help the marketing agency determine how to present the advertisements.

Here, we've used a data set with ten factors, including daily time spent on the site, age, gender, city, quantity of internet usage, and clicked ads. The most significant variable in this case is "clicked on ad," which also serves as our output variable. The clicked ad variable has two possible values: 0 or 1. This suggests that there are two possible output classes: 0 for the user not to click the advertisement and 1 for the user to click the commercial.

Nine more variables comprise our input variables, which work together to help us anticipate the output class. The goal is to analyze which factors should be used to.

train our machine learning model and how they interact to influence the user's choice to click the advertisement.

## 5 Implementation and Results

The dataset used to develop the model contains numerous null values. Null values significantly increase the likelihood of misclassification, so we must eliminate them. To do this, we must process the data set with Pandas and NumPy.

We turn the provided CSV file into a data frame called data. Using the info function of the Pandas data frame, we can determine the data type, the number of records, and whether or not a column is null.

Our primary objective is to count the null values in each column. This ostensibly challenging assignment may be completed quickly using the Pandas package's ISNA () and sum() methods. We must then find the number of null values and re- place each one with a suitable value. The simplest solution is changing it to the mean or median values in the column. Using the data. Mean () and data.median() functions, the mean, and the median are determined. The fill () function is used to fill the null values. We can use either the mean or the median to replace the null values. However, the median might be preferable in some situations, such as age, which cannot be expressed in decimals.

We use the most frequent string to replace null values in columns with string values. To figure this out, we utilize the value counts() method, which returns the string's count. The fill () function is then used to replace null values.

After preprocessing our data, we will assess the correlation between the columns and plot it on a heatmap. We can examine the degree of association between differ- ent variables and the "clicked on ad" variable from the heatmap (output variable).

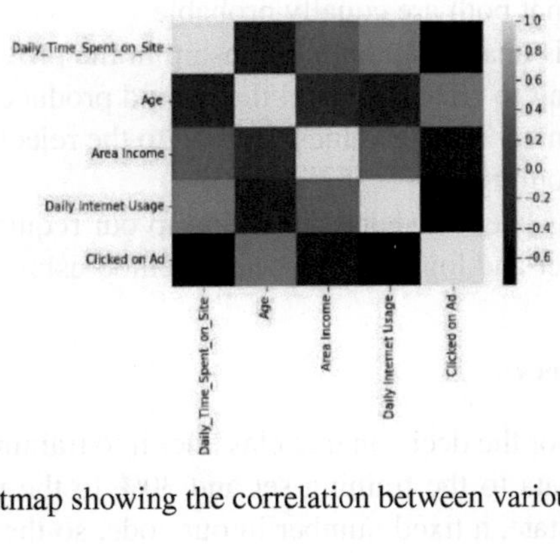


**Fig.1.** Heatmap showing the correlation between various variables.

Figure 1 depicts the correlation between various variables used in our dataset. The higher the correlation, the more impact that variable will have on the target variable (clicked-on ad). The figure shows that Daily time spent on site and internet usage are the two main variables that impact the clicked-on ad variable.

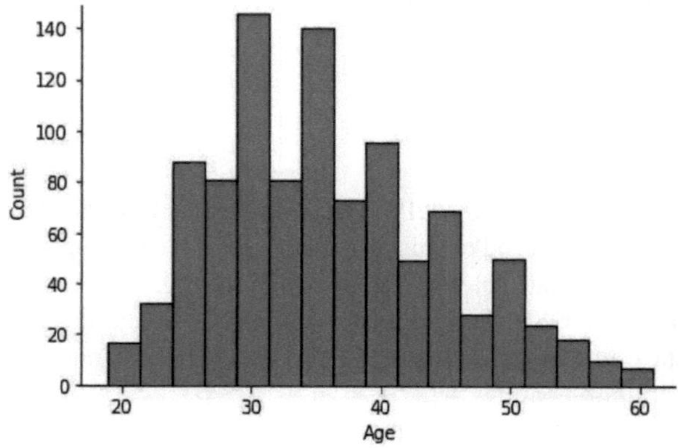


**Fig.2.** Histogram Plot for Daily Time Spent on Site

The histogram depicts the number of users for a particular age group. We can plot similar histograms for all the variables.

We may also use a joint plot to plot two quantities on the same graph to study the relationship between the two variables. Join Plot correlates two variables of our dataset. Figure 2 shows the area income for a particular age group.

Using a pair plot, we can examine the relationship between each variable in the data set and the advertisement's click-through variable. Using different graphs, Fig. 3 shows the relationship between the daily time spent, age, area income, and daily internet usage variables. The dark red color indicates whether the user has clicked on the ad. Similarly, the light red indicates that the user has not clicked on the ad.

When we determine the number of 1s and 0s in the dataset, we find that they are almost equal, meaning that both are equally probable.

A model's key task is analyzing the relationship in the provided data. Therefore, it will be highly challenging to create a model that would produce accurate predictions if the columns contained many unique values, leading to the rejection of columns such as ad topic line, city, and country.

Thus, our dataset has been modeled according to our requirements. We will apply the decision tree classifier and logistic regression method using Skitlearn.

### 5.1 Using Decision Trees

We divided the data set for the decision tree classifier into training and testing sub- sets, allocating 70% of the data to the training set and 30% to the test set. Additional- ly, we specified a random state, a fixed number in our code, so the values in the train and test datasets will always be the same regardless of how much we execute the code. As a

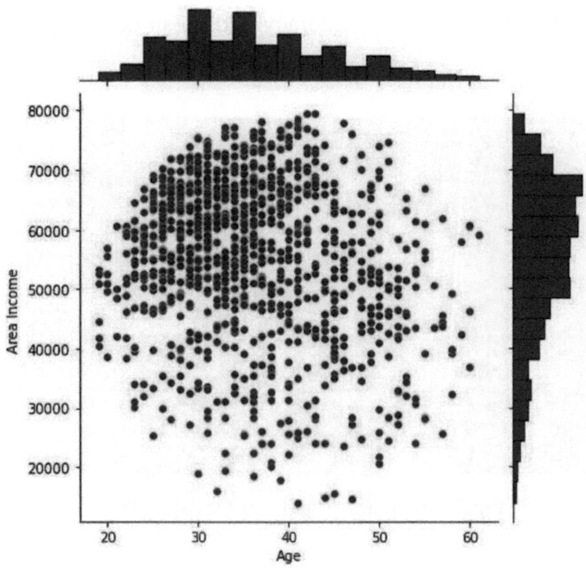


**Fig.3.** Joint Plot between Area Income and Age

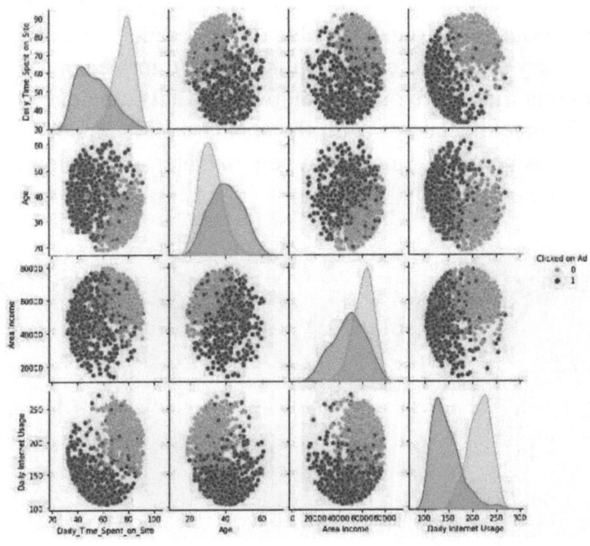


**Fig.4.** Pair Plot for the relationship of all variables to the target variable

result, the outcome will be the same. After that, we predicted the data using the Decision Tree Classifier, which we had imported from the Sklearn library.

Using the sklearn library's functions, we then determined the accuracy scores of the train and test data, the test data's f1 score, and the confusion matrix. Additionally, we determined the standard deviation of accuracy and mean accuracy score using cross-validation.

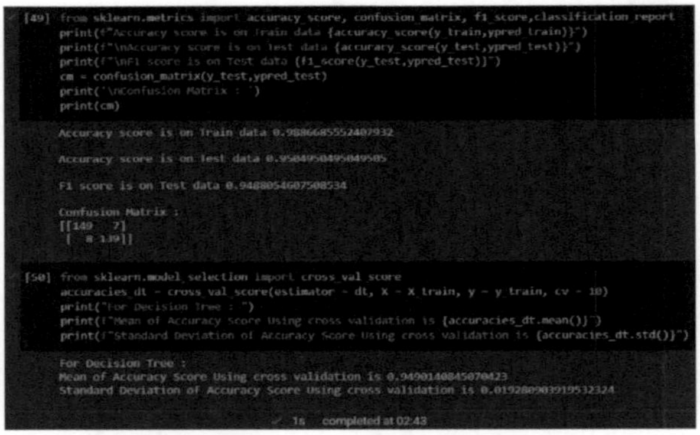


**Fig.5.** Accuracy Report for Decision Tree

### 5.2 Using Logistic Regression

We applied the exact train and test sets for logistic regression, as we used for the decision tree classifier. We fitted and predicted the data using Logistic Regression, which was imported from the Sklearn package. We also displayed the categorization report and calculated the accuracy score and confusion matrix. We implemented the 'newton-cg' hyperparameter tuning method to our model to improve its efficiency because we were only getting 90.42 percent accuracy with the standard LoR model. We then followed the same procedure as before. Using the hyperparameter, we achieved an accuracy of 96.03%.

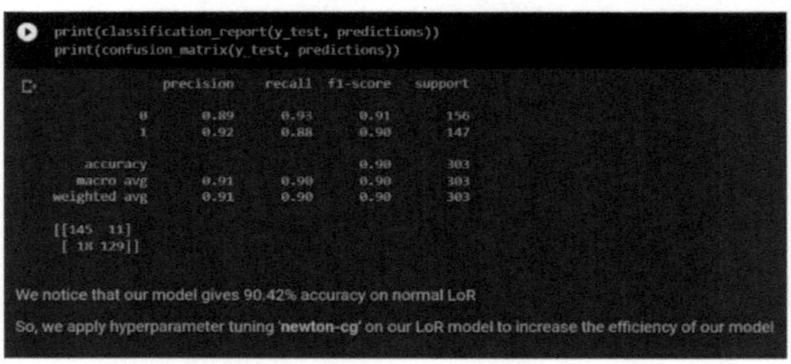


**Fig.6.** Accuracy Report for Logistic Regression

## 6 Conclusion

In this paper, we have first analyzed various target selection methods, which are multiple methods by which we can implement the concept of targeted advertising. We have also shown cross-validation as one of the methods to measure the relative difference of metrics for the models under consideration. On analyzing the data with different models, Decision Trees, and Logistic Regression, we got the mean accuracy score of the decision tree as 0.93, whereas that of Logistic regression was 0.90. We have used a confusion matrix to calculate the performance of various models. F1 score and accuracy calculated from the confusion matrix give a very clear idea about the relative performance of multiple models. However, after applying hyper-tuning parameters to logistic regression, the accuracy was 0.96. Thus, from the above results, we can safely conclude that a decision tree more accurately predicts whether the user will click on the advertisement.

## References


1. Saraswathi, S., Krishnamurthy, V., Prasad, D. V. V., R K, T., Abhinav, S., Rushitaa, D.: Machine learning based ad-click prediction system. Int. J. Eng. Adv. Technol. **8**(6), 3646–3648. Blue Eyes Intelligence Engineering and Sciences Engineering and Sciences Publication - BEIESP. https://doi.org/10.35940/ijeat.f9366.088619
2. Obiedat, R. (2020). Developing decision tree based models in combination with filter feature selection methods for direct marketing. Int. J. Adv. Comput. Sci. Appl. **11**(1). The Science and InformationOrganization. https://doi.org/10.14569/ijacsa.2020.0110180
3. Šoltés, E., Táborecká-Petrovičová, J., Šipoldová, R.: Targeting of online advertising using logistic regression. E+M Ekonomie a Manag. **23**(4), pp. 197–214 (2020). Technical Universityof Liberec. https://doi.org/10.15240/tul/001/2020-4-013
4. Choi, J.-A., Lim, K.: Identifying machine learning techniques for classification of target advertising. ICT Express **6**(3), 175– 180 (2020). Else- vier BV. https://doi.org/10.1016/j.icte.2020.04.012
5. Phaisangittisagul, E., Koobkrabee, Y., Wirojborisuth, K., Ratanasrimetha, T., Aummaro, S. (2019). Target Advertising Classification using a Co, m- b, ination of Deep Learning and Text model. In 2019 10th International Co, n- f, erence of Information and Communication Technology for Embedded Sy, s- t, ems (IC-ICTES): 10th International Conference of Information and Communication Technology for Embedded Systems (IC-ICTES). IEEE (2019). https://doi.org/10.1109/ictemsys.2019.8695956
6. Hany A Elsalamony. Bank direct marketing analysis of data mining tech- niques. International Journal of Computer Applications, 85(7):12–22, 2014
7. Kalmegh, S.: Analysis of Weka data mining algorithm reptree, simple cart and randomtree for classification of Indian news. Int. J. Innov. Sci. Eng. Technol. **2**(2), 438–446 (2015)
8. Wei Li, Xuemei Wu, Yayun Sun, and Quanju Zhang. Credit card customer segmentation and target marketing based on data mining. In 2010 International Con- ference on Computational Intelligence and Security, pages 73–76. IEEE, 2010
9. Mitik, M., Korkmaz, O., Karagoz, P., Toroslu, I. H., Yucel, F.: Data mining based product marketing technique for banking products. In: 2016 IEEE 16t International Conference on Data Mining Workshops (ICDMW), pp. 552–559. IEEE (2016)
10. Chapelle, O., Manavoglu, E., Rosales, R.: Simple and scalable response prediction for display advertising. ACM Trans. Intell. Syst. Technol. TIST **5**(4), 61 (2015)
11. Li, C., Lu, Y., Mei, Q., Wang, D., Pandey, S.: Click-through prediction for advertising in Twitter timeline, pp. 1959–1968 (2015)
12. B. Dalessandro, F. Provost, T. Raeder, C. Per- lich, and O. Stitelman, Ma- chine learning for targeted display advertising: Transfer learning in action, 2013
13. Dansana, D., Patro, S.G.K., Mishra, B.K., Prasad, V., Razak, A., Wodajo, A.W.: Analyzing the impact of loan fea- tures on bank loan prediction using Random Forest algorithm. Wiley, In Engineering Re- ports (2023). https://doi.org/10.1002/eng2.12707

14. Dansana, D., Adhikari, J. D., Mohapatra, M., Sahoo, S.: An approach to analyse and Forecast Social media data using machine learning and data analysis. In: 2020 International Conference on Computer Science, Engineering and Applications (ICCSEA). 2020 International Conference on Computer Science, Engineering and Applications(ICCSEA), IEEE (2020). https://doi.org/10.1109/iccsea49143.2020.9132895
15. Dansana, D., Sahoo, S., Ashraf, F., Kumar Prasad, V., Das, K.:. Machine learning approach to exploratory data analysis on global terrorism. In: Lecture Notes in Networks and Systems, (pp. 623–640). Springer Nature Singapore (2022). https://doi.org/10.1007/978-981-19-1412-6_54
16. Prasad, V. K., Dansana, D., Patro, S. G. K., Salau, A. O., Yadav, D., Bhavsar, M.: CIA-CVD: cloud based image analysis for COVID-19 vaccination distribution. J. Cloud Comput. **12**(1). Springer Science and Business Media LLC (2023). https://doi.org/10.1186/s13677-023-00539-y

# Customer Behavior Analysis Using Loss Function in Federated Machine Learning: A Comparison Analysis

Souvik Pal(✉), Tanmoy Das, Souradeep De, Mitodru Ghosh, and Ipsita Sannyashi

Department of Computer Science and Engineering, Sister Nivedita University (Techno India Group), Kolkata, India
Souvikpal22@gmail.com

**Abstract.** To thrive in today's data-driven market, companies must master the art of consumer behaviour analysis. This study explores Federated Machine Learning (FML), a technique that enables machine learning on decentralized customer data, ensuring privacy. We compare the performance of various algorithms within FML for customer behavior analysis using a bank dataset. Our evaluation metrics include accuracy, precision, and log loss. Random Forest outperforms other algorithms, achieving the highest accuracy, precision, and lowest log loss, making it a reliable choice for customer behavior prediction in FML environments. This study paves the way for future research on scalability, real-world application testing, and the impact of federated learning protocols on model performance.

**Keywords:** Behavior analysis · Loss Function · Federated Machine Learning

## 1 Introduction

In today's rapidly advancing landscape of data analytics and machine learning, understanding customer behavior has become essential for businesses striving to stay ahead in a competitive market. As consumers increasingly engage with digital platforms, the volume of data generated offers unprecedented opportunities for insights and strategic decision-making. Analyzing customer behavior not only helps in making informed decisions but also add value of the role in optimizing the market strategies and overall customer experiences. This comprehensive study focuses on customer behavior analysis through the lens of Federated Machine Learning (FML) [1, 2], a cutting-edge approach that enables machine learning on decentralized data while maintaining data privacy and security. We explore the effectiveness of various algorithms within this framework, aiming to shed light on their performance and practical implications. Federated learning represents in the way that machine learning models are trained and deployed using a paradigm shift. Traditional machine learning concepts require aggregating all data in a central repository, which can raise significant role in privacy and security. Federated learning, on the other hand, its allow models to be trained between multiple decentralized


R. Kumar et al. (Eds.): ICNGCCA 2025, LNICST 665, pp. 15–24, 2026.
https://doi.org/10.1007/978-3-032-13009-9_2

servers hold local data samples without the need to transfer the data to a central server [1]. This concept is not only enhances data privacy but it also leverages the computational power of edge devices [12, 13], leading to more scalable and efficient machine learning solutions customer behavior analysis [4] [5] has evolved significantly over the past few decades. Initially, businesses relied on simple statistical methods and basic data collection techniques to understand consumer preferences and behaviors. However, with this big data and sophisticated machine learning algorithms, the scope and accuracy of customer behavior analysis have expanded dramatically. Modern techniques allows for the processing and analysis of vast amount of data from various sources, including social media, transaction records and web browsing patterns. This holistic approach enables businesses to gain deeper insights into customer preferences, predict future behaviors, and tailor their offerings accordingly.

### 1.1 Significance of the Study

This study bridges the gap between Federated Machine Learning (FML) theory and practical applications in customer behavior analysis. We demonstrate FML's effectiveness using a bank dataset for financial customer behavior analysis while maintaining data privacy. Our contributions include advancements in FML, business strategy through actionable customer insights, and a comparative analysis of machine learning algorithms within the FML framework. This real-world application serves as a blueprint for other industries to leverage FML for data analytics and improved operational strategies.

### 1.2 Objectives of the Work

The primary objective of this study is to leverage Federated Machine Learning (FML) to analyze customer behavior and compare the performance of different machine learning algorithms within this framework. Specifically, we aim to implement federated learning by training models on decentralized data while ensuring data security and privacy. To gauge the overall soundness of the models, their capacity to detect positive occurrences, and their predictive potential, we will measure their performance using metrics like recall, accuracy, precision, and binary cross-entropy/log loss. Additionally, we aim to advance FML techniques by applying them to customer behavior analysis, demonstrating their practical application. This includes providing actionable business insights to enhance services and marketing strategies and offering guidance on the most effective algorithms for customer behavior analysis in a decentralized setting.

## 2 Literature Review

In this section, we have discussed Background study of the work. In their study, Gull and Pervaiz [3] examined the behaviour of individuals who visit online shopping websites and spend their time browsing for various items. The number of individuals present and the proportion of them engaged in shopping would also be considered. This study applies several queries to extract data from a certain website's database, enabling the investigation of client behaviour in relation to online buying. To categorise and analyse the features of consumer moving path process logs, M. Liu et al. [4] used the K-medoids technique, which is based on the Levenshtein distance. Additionally, by studying the paths taken by various types of customers when shopping using PM technology, they were able to perform correlation analysis. Khade, A. A. [5] suggested the use of Map Reduce to create the C4.5 decision tree algorithm, a widely used statistical classifier. In addition, the system aspires to incorporate Customer data visualisation utilising Data Driven Documents, enabling us to create highly tailored visualisations. M. Thabet [6] conducted an analysis of the current techniques used to forecast customer behaviour, as well as identified the various forms of federated learning and their appropriate applications in different scenarios. This study offers a thorough depiction of approaches used to forecast client behaviour. A collaborative clustering method has been presented by U. Ahmed et. al. [7] that eliminates the need for exchanging raw data. The attention-based model is employed inside a federated learning framework. S. Pal and his team [8–13] have examined several parameters in Cloud-Edge-IoT setups utilising optimisation techniques and machine learning models. Alejandro G. Martín et. al. [14] have classified existing works into four categories based on several topic-based features: keywords, application domain, Machine Learning technique, and data type. This work seeks to comprehensively analyse the current references, with the goal of promoting the transmission of cutting-edge methodologies and evaluating their strengths and weaknesses. Additionally, it intends to highlight any unresolved difficulties and potential paths for future research. In their study, Y. Chen et al. [15] developed a recommendation model for physical retailers that takes into account both client choice and temporal influence. The experimental results demonstrate the superiority of the proposed approach in both recommending captivating establishments to customers and aiding retailers in gaining a deeper understanding of customer preferences.

## 3 Research Design

In this research design section, the design show that all the research for done this analysis model to do. It is also describe the overview of the model that is build before the implementation part.

### 3.1 Flow Chart

The Fig. 1 is deals with the workflow of the paper/model, defining the all steps for building and steps, how the models process from the initial to the end process.

The exact models steps are show below-

*Step 1:**Start.***

*Step 2:Input customer data.*

*Step 3:Data cleaning for null and unidentified values.*

*Step 4:create a dummy training model.*

*Step 5:Created our comparison model.*

*Step 5.1: Random forest Algorithm.*

*Step 5.1.1: Visualization the algorithm and analysis.*

*Step 5.1.2: Display Value.*

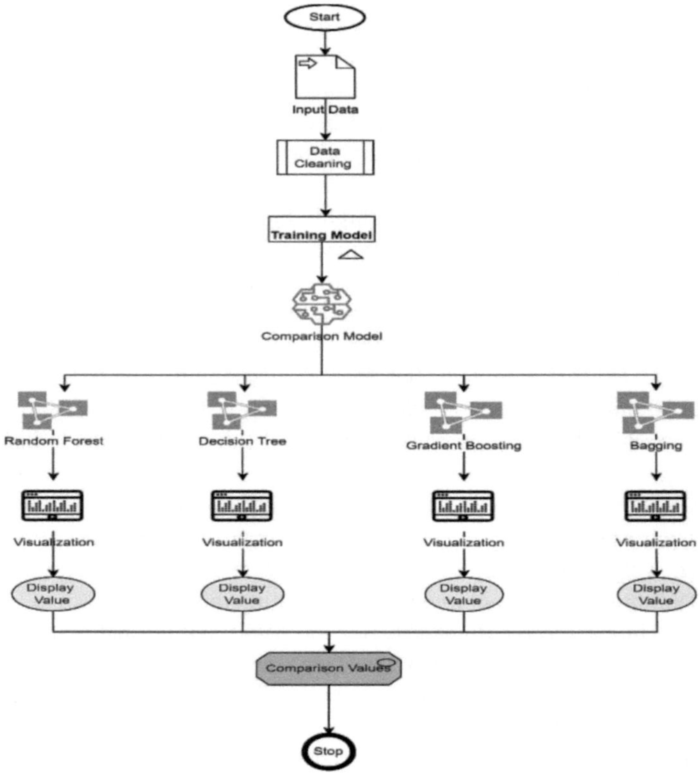


**Fig. 1.** System Structure of the analysis model.

*Step 5.2: Decision Tree Algorithm.*
*Step 5.2.1: Visualization the algorithm and analysis.*
*Step 5.2.2: Display Value.*
*Step 5.3: Gradient Boosting Algorithm.*
*Step 5.3.1: Visualization the algorithm and analysis.*
*Step 5.3.2: Display Value.*
*Step 5.4: Bagging Algorithm.*
*Step 5.4.1: Visualization the algorithm and analysis.*
*Step 5.4.2: Display Value.*
*Step 6:Combining displayed all algorithms values.*
*Step 7:Comparison that all values and finalized.*
*Step 8:**Stop.***
These are the all steps in our models.

## 4 Comparison Analysis

Comparison analysis section is the analysis for all the models and its displayed values. All the result values with comparison according to some parameter that's are Accuracy, Precision and binary cross- entropy or log loss. Being used that's parameter finalize the final values and comparison on that values will give the analysis result which algorithms is best.

### 4.1 Accuracy

Accuracy is a measure in machine learning that can assess the frequency with which a model or algorithm accurately predicts the outcome. By taking the total number of guesses and dividing it by the number of right predictions.

$$Accuray = \frac{TP + TN}{TP + TN + FP + FN}$$

TP is for True Positives, TN stands for True Negatives, FP stands for False Positives, and FN stands for False Negatives. This allows for the identification of every possible scenario.

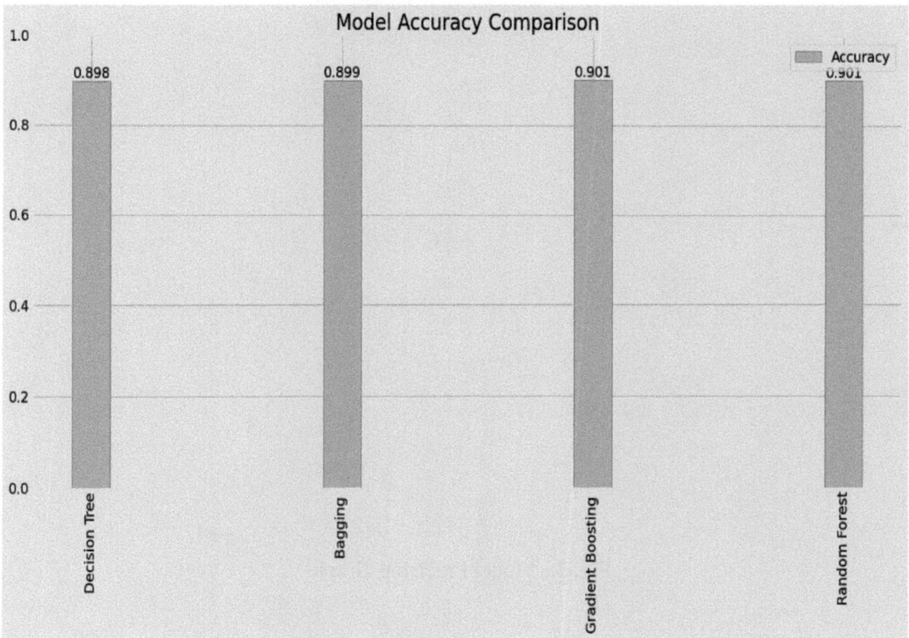


**Fig. 2.** Model Accuracy Graph

In Fig. 2, we can see that Random Forest classifier has the high accuracy from all the algorithms which is 0.902000 then, the Gradient Boosting = 0.901000, then Bagging Classifier = 0.899000.

### 4.2 Precision

In the field of machine learning, precision is a statistic that may be used to quantify the frequency with which a machine learning model or algorithm accurately predicts the positive class out of all the classes that are predicted. When we talk about precision, we are referring to the number of true positives class divided by the overall number of predictions generated by the model, which includes both the true positives and the false positives themselves.

$$Precision = \frac{TruePositives}{TruePositives + FalsePositive}$$

If you think, that can measure the precision in a scale range between 0 to 1%. When precision is higher, precision is better for that model, and when is lower, precision value is lower for that model. When precision is 1.0% the model is always right to predicting the target class.

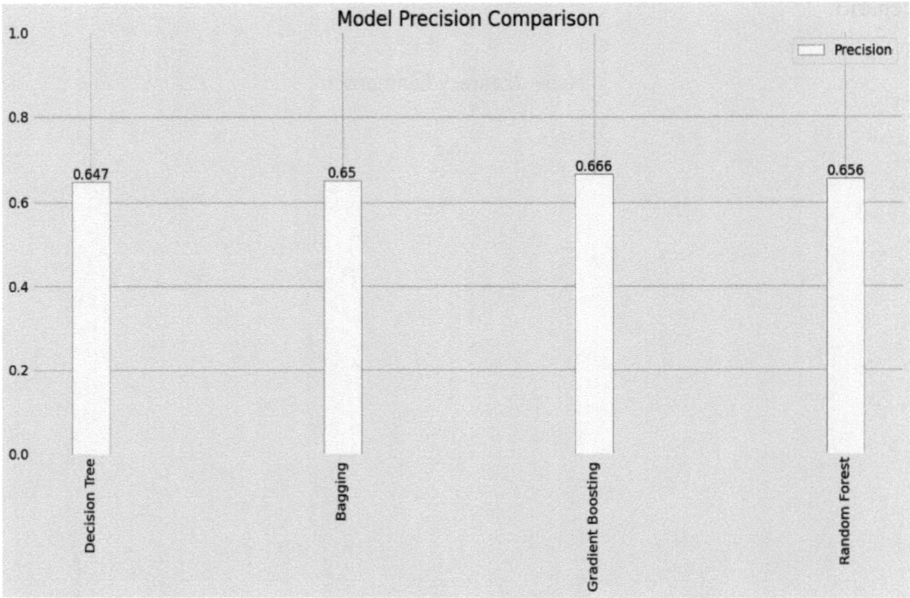


**Fig. 3.** Model Precision Graph

In our comparison analysis in Fig. 3, we can observe that Gradient Boosting has the highest Precision which is 0.666000, followed closely by the random forest = 0.656000, then Bagging = 0.650000.

### 4.3 Loss Function and Binary Cross-Entropy Loss (Log Loss)

In machine learning, federated learning is the part of optimizing the models where the local model is obtained by optimizing the loss function or loss value of the local data, in other hand global model is obtaining by the aggregating of the local models are participating in the training.

In machine learning, our main purpose is to find a model for training our decentralized data that can minimize the loss function of that newly learned model distribution differs from the empirical distribution.

$$BCE(y\_true, y\_pred) = -(y\_true * log(y\_pred) + (1 - y\_true) * log(1 - y\_pred))$$

where *y_true* is the true label for a data point, *y_pred* is the predicted models assigns to the positive class and log is the natural logarithm.

**Loss Function.** Loss function is generally knows as error function, it is a crucial component in machine learning models that finds the error between different machine learning algorithm's predicted outputs and the actual target values. Two major categories of loss functions highlight classification and regression difficulties. Classifications require predicting all class probabilities. Regression in machine learning algorithms predicts continuous values using independent features.

**Binary Cross-Entropy.** A model measure known as binary cross entropy, sometimes known as log loss, is used to monitor and identify instances of improper labelling of the data class. If the log loss value is low, then the accuracy values will also be high. Binary cross entropy is equal to the $-1 * log(likelihood)$.

$-\frac{1}{N}\sum_{i=1}^{N} y_i.log(p(y_i)) + (1 - y_i).log(1 - p(y_i))$

Here, the actual class is represents $Yi$, $log(p(yi))$ is the probability of that class.

And $N$ is the number of rows.

Here is the log loss model graph below:

In Fig. 4, we can analysis that less log loss value means that algorithms has the lowest data loss. So, here Random Forest has the lowest, and then gradient boosting, then bagging and lastly decision tree.

### 4.4 Comparison Different Values

After all the observation, the results show that the comparison difference between the four algorithms (decision tree, random forest, bagging, and gradient boosting) are well enough to find customer behavior according to the provided dataset. Random forest classifiers have the highest accuracy and precision and also have the lowest number of log loss or errors in the data, so on.

The comparative model graph is shown below (Fig. 5):

Fig. 4 Analysis that for our customer behavior analysis random forest and gradient boosting is the best for our models.

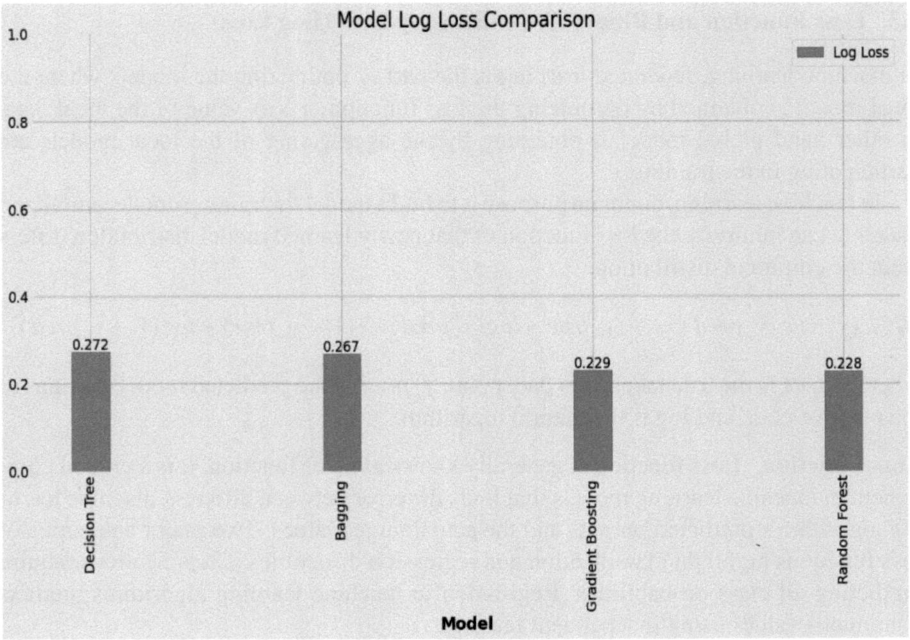


**Fig. 4.** Model Log Loss Graph.

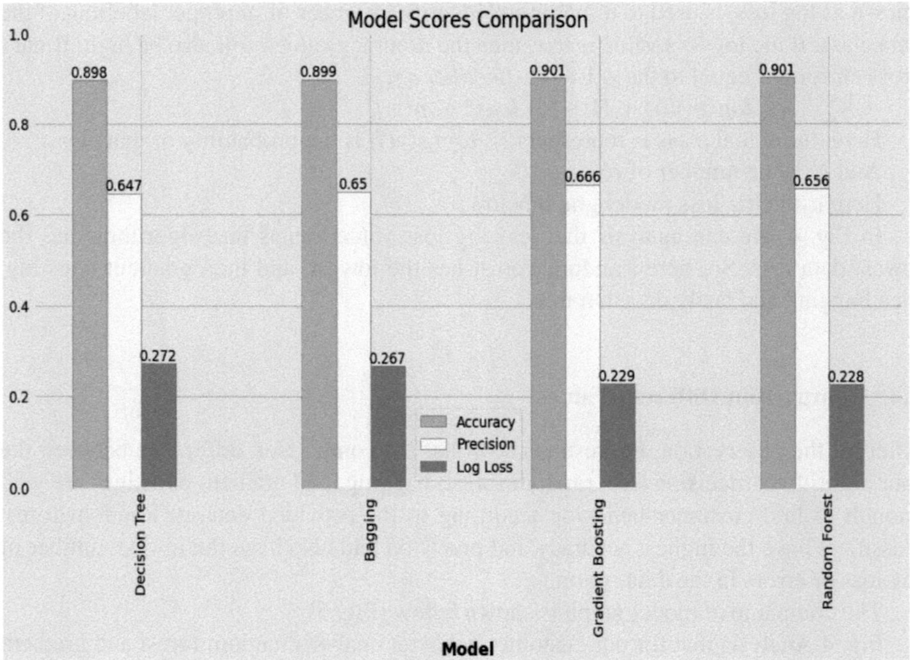


**Fig. 5.** Comparison values of all the algorithms.

## 5 Conclusion and Future Works

This in-depth study explored customer behavior through Federated Machine Learning (FML), evaluating various machine learning algorithms within this privacy-preserving framework. To gain actionable customer insights, we meticulously cleaned and analyzed a bank dataset using FML techniques. By comparing algorithms based on accuracy, precision, and log loss, we found Random Forest, Gradient Boosting, and Bagging to be highly effective for FML-based customer behavior analysis. Random Forest emerged as the leader with superior accuracy and minimal errors, making it a reliable choice for customer behavior prediction. While Gradient Boosting and Bagging offered strong performance through ensemble methods, Random Forest's exceptional results suggest its potential to improve marketing strategies and customer satisfaction through highly accurate predictions. Future research will focus on scalability and efficiency to ensure these algorithms handle growing datasets, along with real-world application testing to understand integration challenges and evaluate the impact of different FML protocols on model performance and training efficiency.

## References

1. Banabilah, S., Aloqaily, M., Alsayed, E., Malik, N., Jararweh, Y.: Federated learning review: Fundamentals, enabling technologies, and future applications. Info. Process. Amp Manag. **59**(6), 103061 (2022). Elsevier BV. https://doi.org/10.1016/j.ipm.2022.103061
2. Wang, Y., Ma, J., Gao, N., Wen, Q., Sun, L., Guo, H.: Federated fuzzy k-means for privacy-preserving behavior analysis in smart grids. Appl. Energy **331**, 120396 (2023). https://doi.org/10.1016/j.apenergy.2022.120396
3. Gull, M., Pervaiz, A.: Customer behavior analysis towards online shopping using data mining. In: 2018 5th International Multi-Topic ICT Conference (IMTIC), Jamshoro, Pakistan, pp. 1–5 (2018). https://doi.org/10.1109/IMTIC.2018.8467262
4. Liu, M., Zhao, L., Sun, F., Zhao, W., Zuo Y., Yada, K.: Customer behavior analysis and classification based on process mining. In: 2021 IEEE International Conference on Systems, Man, and Cybernetics (SMC), Melbourne, Australia, pp. 1000–1005 (2021). https://doi.org/10.1109/SMC52423.2021.9659063
5. Khade, A. A.: Performing customer behavior analysis using big data analytics. Proc. Comput. Sci. **79**, 986–992 (2016). Elsevier BV. https://doi.org/10.1016/j.procs.2016.03.125
6. Thabet, M., Messaadia, M., Kumar, M.: Distributed machine learning for predicting customer behavior while preserving privacy. In: *2023 International Conference on Decision Aid Sciences and Applications (DASA)*, Annaba, Algeria, pp. 613–617 (2023). https://doi.org/10.1109/DASA59624.2023.10286716
7. Ahmed, U., Lin, J. C. -W., Srivastava, G: Deep-attention model to analyze reliable customers via federated learning. In: 2021 International Joint Conference on Neural Networks (IJCNN), Shenzhen, China, 2021, pp. 1–7 (2021). https://doi.org/10.1109/IJCNN52387.2021.9533486
8. Chander, B., Pal, S., De, D., Buyya, R.: Artificial intelligence-based internet of things for industry 5.0. In: Pal, S., De, D., Buyya, R. (eds) Artificial Intelligence-based Internet of Things Systems. Internet of Things. Springer, Cham (2022). https://doi.org/10.1007/978-3-030-87059-1_1
9. Pal, S., Jhanjhi, N.Z., Abdulbaqi, A.S., Akila, D., Alsubaei, F.S., Almazroi, A.A.: An intelligent task scheduling model for hybrid internet of things and cloud environment for big data applications. Sustainability **15**, 5104 (2023). https://doi.org/10.3390/su15065104

10. Tuan, Nguyen A., D. Akila, Souvik Pal, Bikramjit Sarkar, Thien Khai Tran, G. Mothilal Nehru, and Dac-Nhuong Le. "Dynamic data optimization in IoT-assisted sensor networks on cloud platform. Comput. Mater. Continua **72**(1) (2022).https://doi.org/10.32604/cmc.2022.024096
11. Pal, S., VijayKumar, H., Akila, D., Jhanjhi, N. Z., Darwish, O. A., Amsaad, F.: Information-centric IoT-based smart farming with dynamic data optimization. Comput. Mater. Continua, **74**(2) (2023).https://doi.org/10.32604/cmc.2023.029038
12. Mukherjee, D., et al.: Optimized energy efficient strategy for data reduction between edge devices in cloud-IoT. Comput. Mater. Cont. **72**(1) (2022).https://doi.org/10.32604/cmc.2022.023611
13. Pal, S., Jhanjhi, N.Z., Abdulbaqi, A.S., Akila, D., Almazroi, A.A., Alsubaei, F.S.: A Hybrid edge-cloud system for networking service components optimization using the internet of things. Electronics **12**(3), 649 (2023). https://doi.org/10.3390/electronics12030649
14. G. Martín, A., Fernández-Isabel, A., Martín de Diego, I. et al.: A survey for user behavior analysis based on machine learning techniques: current models and applications. Appl. Intell. **51**, 6029–6055 (2021). https://doi.org/10.1007/s10489-020-02160-x
15. Chen, Y., Zheng, Z., Chen, S., Sun, L., Chen, D.: Mining customer preference in physical stores from interaction behavior. IEEE Access **5**, 17436–17449 (2017). https://doi.org/10.1109/ACCESS.2017.2744263

# Method Level Refactoring Prediction Using CodeBERT Model

Archana Patnaik[1(✉)], Neelamadhab Padhy[1], Lov Kumar[2], and Rasmita Panigrahi[1]

[1] Department of CSE, GIET University, Gunupur, Odisha, India
{archanapatnaik,dr.neelamadhab,rasmita}@giet.edu

[2] Department of CE, NIT, Kurukshetra, Haryana, India
lovkumar@nitkkr.ac.in

**Abstract.** CodeBERT is an autoencoder model used for code search, code synthesis and classification. It is to improve the code quality by handling large amounts of codebases. As it operates on two natural languages, it is considered as bimodal. Objectives: In this work we have used this model for generating automated refactoring suggestions at method level by using java code snippets.Materials and Methods: Our works focuses on the details implementation of automated model which is used for refactoring prediction. Binary labels are used for synthesizing the code snippets which is classified in two category that is high probability and low probability refactoring. Result Analysis: Code analysis is done on five different java code snippets that is related to method level refactoring category. CodeBERT model performed refactoring prediction using the labels and the analysis is done by using snippets related to extract method, inline method, rename method, move method and pull up method techniques. Performance of the pre-trained model for snippet 4 is high with accuracy 97%, precision 0.98, recall 0.98 and f-measure 0.98 respectively.Conclusion: CodeBERT model gives good results for java code snippets with maximum accuracy of 97%. Refactoring suggestions provided by the model helps to identify the requirement of code alteration which is highly beneficial to the code developer.

**Keywords:** Refactoring · CodeBERT · Deep Learning · Software Quality

## 1 Introduction

Recent emerging technologies in the field of software engineering demands the product quality assurance using automated tools and pre trained models. As the software systems deals with massive amount of data, it is quite impossible to conduct the assessment manually. In order to overcome the drawbacks of the existing tools and technologies, various machine learning model are used for assessing the code structure contributing towards the quality improvement which is done by restructuring. BERT based deep learning model are used for detecting code smell and predicting refactoring using code snippets. The extension of BERT [1, 2] models termed as RefBERT that is compiled to predict the restructuring using software metrics on GLUE benchmark dtasets. This


R. Kumar et al. (Eds.): ICNGCCA 2025, LNICST 665, pp. 25–34, 2026.
https://doi.org/10.1007/978-3-032-13009-9_3

pre trained framework is implemented on automatic rename refactoring that is done in two stages (i) Predicts number of tokens and sub tokens (ii) Identifies bag of token loss. Enhancement of code snippets through natural language highly contributes towards Neural code search which deals with annotated set of queries for NLP transfer learning models. In our research work we have used CodeBERT pre trained model for assuring the quality of code developed by the software developers. It is a multi-programming lingual model developed used six natural language and programming languages basically used for performing different tasks like code optimization, code summarization, code translation, code completion etc. For code snippets quality [3] checking deep learning generative models are used by evaluating Levenshtein distance and BLEU score. The prime advantage of this model is that it can be used for repairing [6] bugs of automated simple java programming by using the concept of sequence-to-sequence learning. This model is transformer based neural network architecture that incorporates [7] hybrid tasks like tokenization, token detection, token generation and predicting BERT score based on reference code. CodeBERT is considered as the bimodal extensions of BERT model that takes both natural languages and source code as input.

In the golden era of deep learning many researchers have implemented Convolution Neural Network (CNN), Long Short Term Memory (LSTM) and Auto encoder based model for dealing with different tasks related to source code. For construct mask of code automated partially generated codes [10] are used at token levels. In order to detect clone unseen code are fine-tuned using java clone pairs for general purpose representations of trained datasets. JavaBERT uses masked language for retrieving data pipeline on java source code with high accuracy. Most commonly used transformer [11] models are RoBERT, GPT, BERT, GPT 2 and RoBERT-a that is used for short description of code. Many pre-trained models are also used for severity code smell detection focusing on software maintainability characteristics. Different types of BERT model are implemented using DJANGO and CoNaLa datasets that is used for modeling casual programming language with minimum BLEU score and maximum accuracy.

CodeBERT score [14] is used for evaluating the performance of generated code which can be either high or low with minimum and maximum performance. Natural language is also used for code evaluation that is labeled in terms of annotated datasets downloaded for Hugging Face hub.

In the experimental survey object-oriented metrics are taken in to consideration from which God class [16] code smell is detected which is further implemented by using brain class and brain method techniques. In deep learning model the labeled training dataset is passed into convolution layer, flatten layer and dense layer Software code quality can be assured by the presence of code smell measured in terms of clean code and dirty code. The novel approach to used ensemble feature [18] selection is already implemented on the metrics-based data which detects the presence of code smell for Random Forest classifier and many other ensemble aggregators like ET6C2, ET5C2 and ET5C1 are used.

## 2 Related Work

Refactoring targets to improve the maintainability and quality of open-source real-time projects by considering its software metrics. Wei et al.,[1] identified the challenging issues of automated rename refactoring using RefBERT that generates the new name for sub tokenizing the variables. They proposed a model considers code snippets as input and generates contextual vector as output each token. Wang et al., [2] facilitates a pre-computed BERT for regulating the interaction of teacher and student model. Their result analysis highlights the accuracy of TinyBERT is 8.1% more than RefBERT that is 94% accuracy. Cinselli et al.,[3] identified several deep learning models for understanding the granularity levels of code. They proposed a RoBERT model evaluates deep learning generative for perfect predictions. Result analysis represents the solution related to the entire code blocks with 58% simple scenarios and 7% on entire blocks. Pan et al., [4] proposed deep learning-based model like CodeBERT-NT, CodeBERT-PK and CodeBERT-PS for software defect prediction for cross project defect prediction and new patterns identification. Ghodhab et al.,[5] proposed a bi-directional encoder pre-trained model for verifying the changes in the source code using deep neural network for performing the commit classification task. The commits are classified into three categories like perfective, adaptive and corrective and build 1793 labeled dataset for fine grained code changes that contributes toward deep analysis. Software debugging [6] and error identification in normal way is very difficult and time consuming.

Transformer based neural network architecture are used for accurate prediction of simple java bug in the code structure. It is observed that sequence learning with 72% accuracy in long and short methods gives better outcomes. Feng et al.,[7] used a bimodal Natural-Language and Program Language (NL-PL) for design a BERT model that can be used for application code documentation and code search. It can also be used for unimodal data for incorporation token detection. Sausa et al.,[8] used various NLP and Machine Learning for designing a JavaBERT that con- tributes toward assuring the code quality. They designed a data retrieval pipeline with high accuracy on Java source code. Transformer model considers the source code that act as training explicitly that is used to evaluate the final performance. Khanfir et al.,[9] designed a pre trained model for omitting the code token. Code naturalness performs different tasks like code tokenization, code sequencing, model ability checking over non-buddy and buggy ranking code. Smart Shark dataset contains 40 projects with 2510 versions and compares the similarity between predicted and actual code. Code clone detection evaluates [10] the model accuracy performance for unseen code. The first, second and third datasets are derived from BigCloneBench, SemanticCloneBench and Android applications for Type 1 and Type 4 clone with 96% and 100% recall values respectively. Heyman et al.,[11] introduced code search mechanism for code snippet retrieval using Natural Language queries. They created domain specific retrieval model with 20.6% absolute gain for annotated code. For three new search variant Mean Reciprocal Rank (MRR) is 23.96%, 20.6% and 26.4% respectively. Natural Language Processing (NLP) transfer learning model compares the similarities between code description and queries. Soliman et al.,[12] proposed a hybrid model based on LUKE, ELECTRA, ROBERT and BERT that is used for code generation. Dataset considered for improving code quality are CoNaLa and DIANGO with exact match accuracy of 89.34% and 78.50%. BERTMarian model performs tasks like word embedding, layer normalization, dropout and positional embedding. Siddiq et al.,[13] investigated the presence of code smell in three training dataset that is Apps, CodeGlue and Code Clippy.Ten Configuration of fine-grained transformer based model is tuned using 125M parameters are identified with two security patterns. Their work focuses on automated code generation by using common patterns by using problematic code generation tools. Zhou et al.,[14] assessed the quality of code by evaluating its performance using a pre-trained score based CodeBERT model. The proposed model provides higher correlation than the existing model that contain real time data and is associated with Hugging Face. Zhang et al.,[15] used Bidirectional Encoder Representation Transformer (BERT) for representation of source code developed by the programmer. The design and implementation demonstrate the important features of variables and functions used in the code organization. Das et al., [16] illustrated the concept of code smell by using Deep Learning algorithms. The proposed model detected two categories of code smell that is Brain method and Brain Class by using mutually exclusive training data. Marian et al., [17] used hierarchical clustering method for predicting software refactoring at package level which is quite beneficial to the software developers. The framework considers the application class related to uncovered hidden patterns and uses clustered based approach for restructuring the code. The concept of technical debt is tested on three open-source dataset by using Random Forest Classifier [18] and the performance is evaluated by using fMeasure, accuracy, G-mean1 and G-mean2. ETC5C1, ETC5C2 and ET6C2 are aggregated for majority voting analysis that is essential for software bug identification.

Based on the systematic literature survey, we have framed two research question:

**RQ 1: Can we use CodeBERT pre-trained model for re- factoring prediction ?**

We have considered five java code snippets for identifying the requirement of the software refactoring by considering its labels. The evaluation metrics values and graphs are represented in the result analysis part.

**RQ 2: How efficiently CodeBERT model works on code snippets for predicting method level refactoring?**

The efficiency of the pre-trained model are evaluated in the terms of performance matrix and graphical survey. We have plotted the Learning Curve, ROC curve and Precision Recall curve for validating the training snippet data.

## 3 Proposed Research Model

In our work we have done the implementation using CodeBERT model that is used for predicting refactoring at method level. The entire workflow is divided into different phases which is represented in Fig. 1 below:

There are six different phases used to illustrate the detailed working mechanism of the pre-trained model.

Phases 1: Data Collection: Data is collected from the open-source java project which is represented in the form of source code snippets. It is considered as input for the model (Table 1).

**Phase 2: Implementation using CodeBERT model:** The input collect- ed is used for implementing the CodeBERT model. The detailed work- ing mechanism is represented below in Fig. 2:

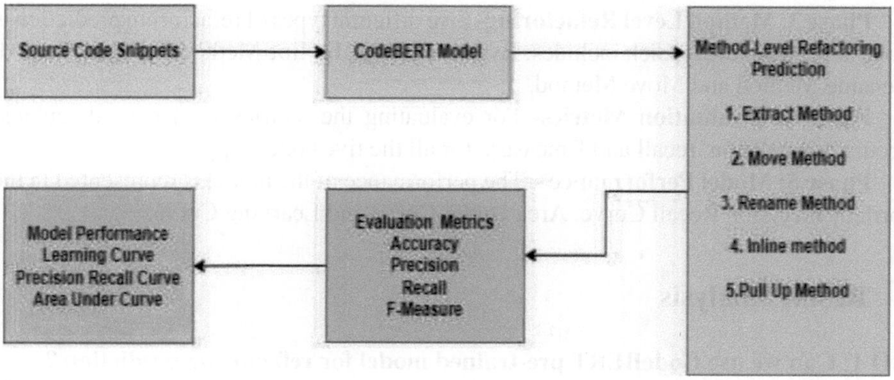


**Fig. 1.** Research Model

**Table 1.** Sample Source Code Snippet

| | |
|---|---|
| **Sample Snippet:**<br>public class order<br>{<br>int item; float tax;<br>double order()<br>{<br>double total = 0; for(n = items) {<br>total = getprice();<br>}<br>doublettax = total + tax;<br>return ttax;<br>}<br>} | **Refactoring Label:** 1<br>**Refactoring Techniques:**<br>Extract Method |

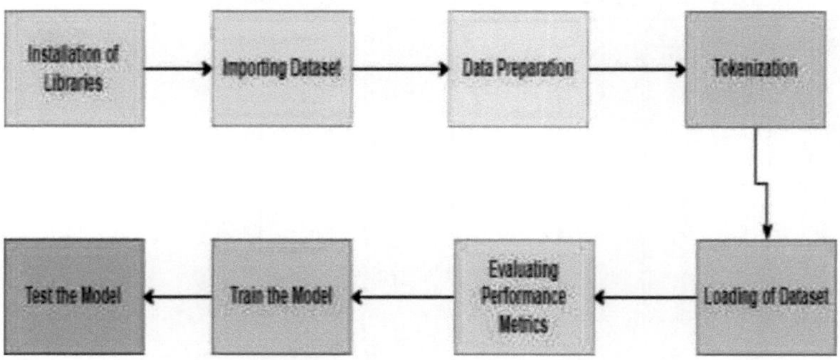


**Fig. 2.** Working Mechanism of CodeBERT Model

**Phase 3: Method Level Refactoring-** Five different types of refactoring prediction is done at method level which includes: Extract Method, In- line Method, Pull Up Method, Rename Method and Move Method.

**Phase 4: Evaluation Metrics-** For evaluating the metrics we have cal- culated accuracy, precision, recall and f-measure for all the five code snippets.

**Phase 5: Model Performance –** The performance of the model is represented in the form of Precision Recall Curve, Area Under Curve and Learning Curve.

## 4 Result Analysis

**RQ 1: Can we use CodeBERT pre-trained model for refactoring prediction ?**

In the result analysis part we have illustrated regarding the implementation of Code-BERT pre-trained model by considering five different input code snippets. We have done the refactoring prediction at method level and the details are represented below in Table 2.

**Table 2.** Performance Evaluation of CodeBERT Model

| Accuracy | Precision | Recall | FMeasure |
|---|---|---|---|
| 92% | 0.94 | 0.94 | 0.94 |
| 88% | 0.88 | 0.88 | 0.88 |
| 93% | 0.93 | 0.93 | 0.93 |
| 97% | 0.98 | 0.98 | 0.98 |
| 82% | 0.84 | 0.84 | 0.84 |

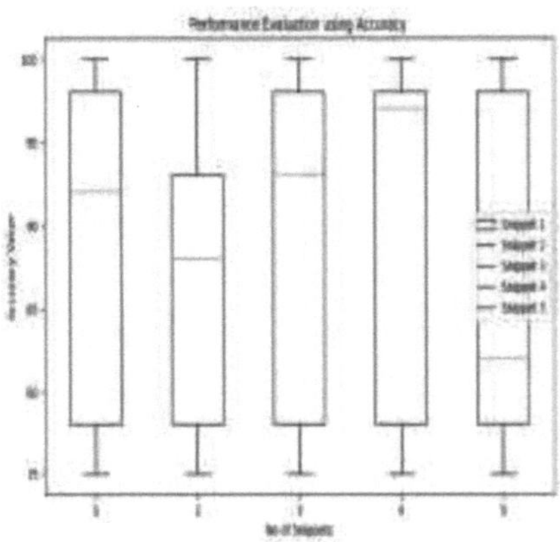

**Fig. 3.** Accuracy

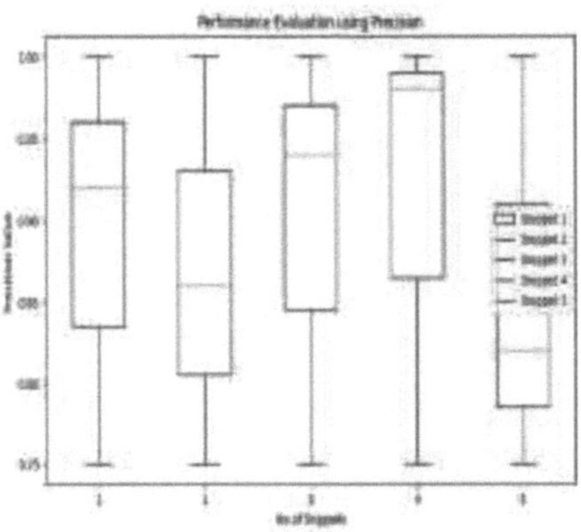

**Fig. 4.** Precision

Figure 3 represents the accuracy of the pre-trained model for five different code snippets. For snippet 1, snippet 2, snippet 3, snippet 4 and snippet 5 the accuracies are 92%, 88%, 93%, 97% and 82% respectively. It is observed that accuracy is high for snippet 4. Figure 4 represents the precision of the pre-trained model for five different code snippets. For snippet 1, snippet 2, snippet 3, snippet 4 and snippet 5 the precision values are 0.94, 0.88, 0.94, 0.98 and 0.84 respectively. It is observed that precision value is high for snippet 4.

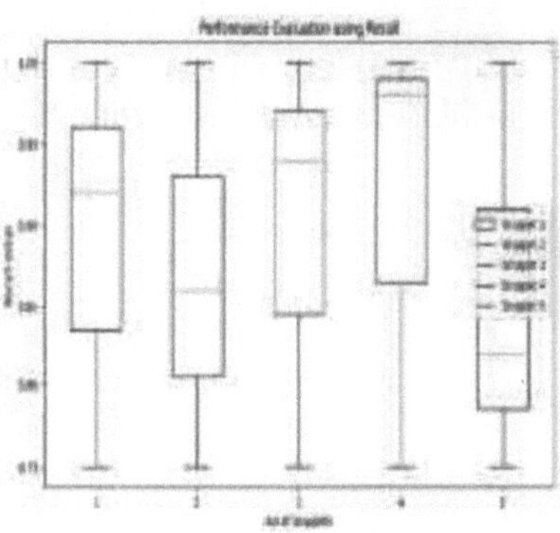

**Fig. 5.** Recall

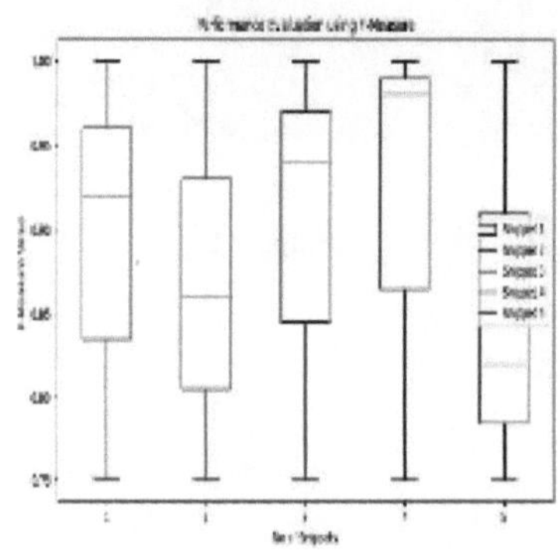

**Fig. 6.** F-Measures

Figure 5 represents the recall of the pre-trained model for five different code snippets. For snippet 1, snippet 2, snippet 3, snippet 4 and snippet 5 the precision values are 0.94, 0.88, 0.94, 0.98 and 0.84 respectively. It is observed that recall value is high for snippet 4.Fig. 6 represents the f-measure of the pre-trained model for five different code snippets. For snippet 1, snippet 2, snippet 3, snippet 4 and snippet 5 the precision values are 0.94, 0.88, 0.94, 0.98 and 0.84 respectively. It is observed that f-measure value is high for snippet 4. For evaluating the performance of the CodeBERT model we have considered the actual and predicted values for finding the confusion matrix for each code snippet which is represented below is Fig. 7. The obtained value for snippet 1, snippet 2, snippet 3, snippet 4 and snippet 5 are represented in different colors and is used for evaluating the performance of the model by considering its data instances.

RQ 2: How efficiently CodeBERT model works on code snippets for predicting method level refactoring?

In our work we have used the encoder based pre-trained for refactoring prediction. In RQ 1 we have evaluated the performance metrics and represented the confusion matrix for all code snippets. For evaluating the time over performance we have used the learning curve which is represented in Fig. 8.

In our work we have used learning Curve to reflect the performance of model based on the training data which is used against the testing data for diagnosing the loss parameters. In x-axis we have represented the training data of code snippet and in y-axis we have the CodeBERT score to compare the training and cross-validation score. We have used Precision-Recall Curve is used to show the area approximation under the curve. As

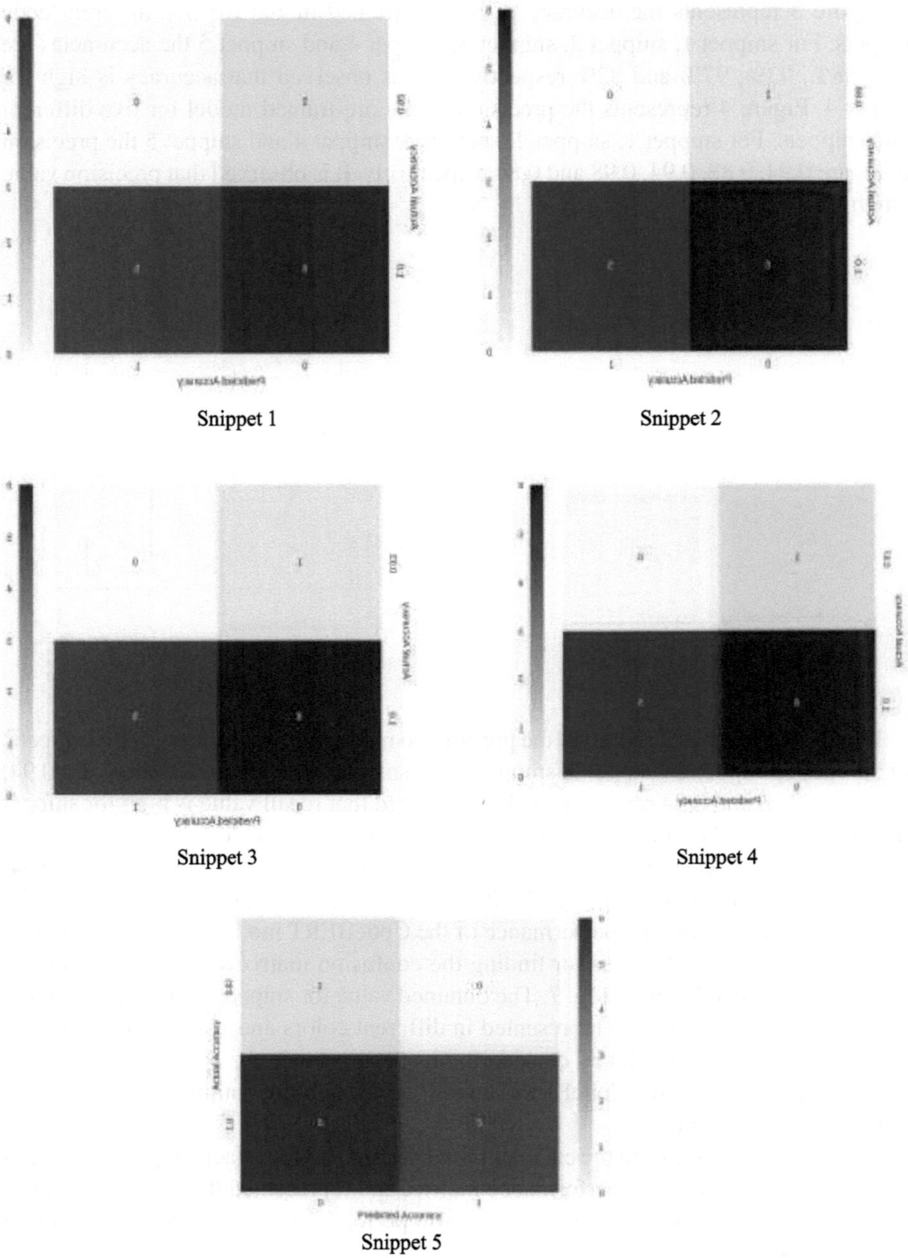


**Fig. 7.** (a) Snippet 1, (b) Snippet 2, (c) Snippet 3, (d) Snippet 4, (e) Snippet 5

snippet 4 is giving good result, so we have used it and average precision obtained is 0.98 which is represented in Fig. 9.

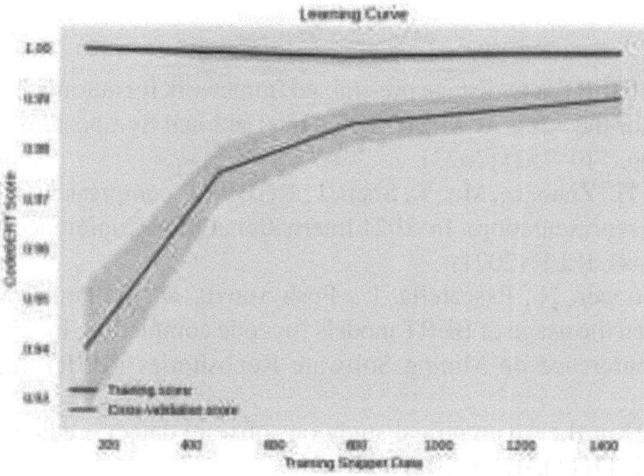

**Fig. 8.** Learning Curve

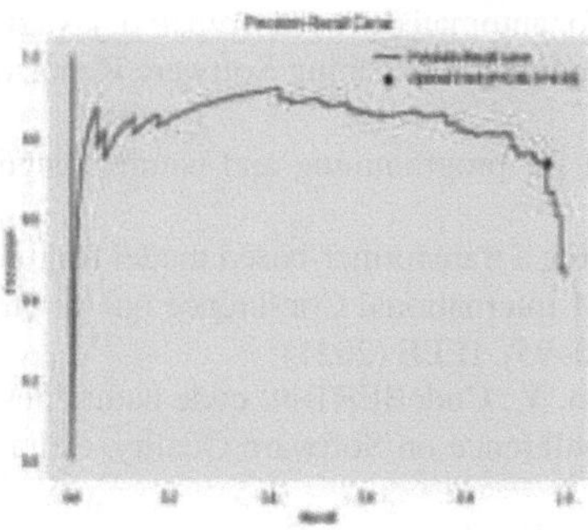

**Fig. 9.** Precision-Recall Curve

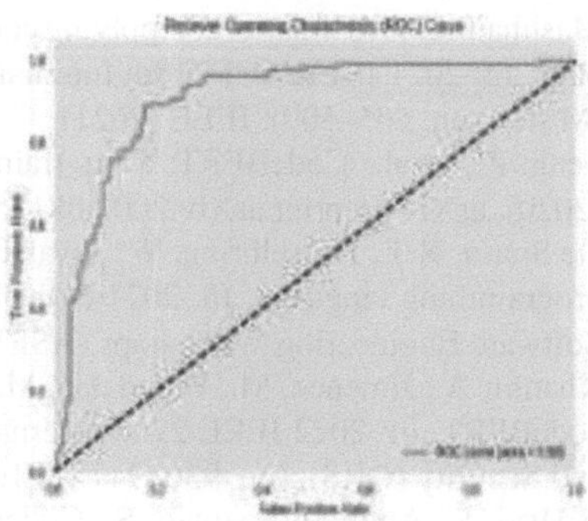

**Fig. 10.** ROC Curve

The above Fig. 10 represent the ROC curve to test and compare the performance of different snippets by considering its True Positive Rate (TPR) and False Positive Rate (FPR). It is observed that the Area Under Curve (AUC) value is highest for snippet 4 that is 0.98.

## 5 Conclusion

In our work, we proposed the novel approach for predicting method level refactoring using CodeBERT pre-trained model by using its labels. Source codes are collected from java projects and implemented for identifying refactoring opportunities. It is highly beneficial to the code developer to restructure the code that is performed in method levels. In our work we have done analysis on extract method, move method, rename method, pull up method and inline method. We have considered 5 source code snippets and performance of snippet 4 is highest with 97% accuracy, precision 0.98, recall 0.98 and f-measure 0.98 respectively. In our future work, we will predict the refactoring on python source code by using different deep learning approaches.

## References


1. Liu, H., et al.: RefBERT: a two-stage pre-trained framework for automatic rename refactoring. In: Proceedings of the 32nd ACM SIGSOFT International Symposium on Software Testing and Analysis, (pp. 740–752) (2023)
2. Wang, X., Yang, H., Zhao, L., Mo, Y., Shen, J.: RefBERT: compressing BERT by referencing to pre-computed representations. In: 2021 International Joint Conference on Neural Networks (IJCNN), (pp. 1–8). IEEE (2021)
3. Ciniselli, M., Cooper, N., Pascarella, L., Poshyvanyk, D., Di Penta, M., Bavota, G.: An empirical study on the usage of BERT models for code completion. In: 2021 IEEE/ACM 18th International Conference on Mining Software Repositories (MSR), (pp. 108–119). IEEE (2021)
4. Pan, C., Lu, M., Xu, B.: An empirical study on software defect prediction using codeBERT model. Appl. Sci. **11**(11), 4793 (2021)
5. Ghadhab, L., Jenhani, I., Mkaouer, M.W., Messaoud, M.B.: Augmenting commit classification by using fine-grained source code changes and a pre-trained deep neural language model. Inf. Softw. Technol. **135**, 106566 (2021)
6. Mashhadi, E., Hemmati, H.: Applying codeBERT for automated program repair of java simple bugs. In: 2021 IEEE/ACM 18th International Conference on Mining Software Repositories (MSR), (pp. 505–509). IEEE (2021)
7. Feng, Z., et al.: CodeBERT: a pre-trained model for programming and natural languages (2020). arXiv preprint arXiv:2002.08155
8. De Sousa, N.T., Hasselbring, W.: JavaBERT: training a transformer-based model for the java programming language. In: 2021 36th IEEE/ACM International Conference on Automated Software Engineering Workshops (ASEW) (pp. 90–95). IEEE (2021)
9. Khanfir, A., Jimenez, M., Papadakis, M., Le Traon, Y.: CodeBERT-nt: code naturalness via codeBERT. In: 2022 IEEE 22nd International Conference on Software Quality, Reliability and Security (QRS), (pp. 936–947). IEEE (2022)
10. Arshad, S., Abid, S., Shamail, S.: CodeBERT for code clone detection: a replication study. In: 2022 IEEE 16th International Workshop on Software Clones (IWSC), (pp. 39–45). IEEE (2022)
11. Heyman, G., Van Cutsem, T.: Neural code search revisited: enhancing code snippet retrieval through natural language intent (2020). arXiv preprint arXiv:2008.12193
12. Soliman, A., Shaheen, S., Hadhoud, M.: Leveraging pre-trained language models for code generation. Complex & Intelligent Systems, pp.1–26 (2024)
13. Siddiq, M.L., Majumder, S.H., Mim, M.R., Jajodia, S. Santos, J. C.: An empirical study of code smells in transformer-based code generation techniques. In: 2022 IEEE 22nd International Working Conference on Source Code Analysis and Manipulation (SCAM), (pp. 71–82). IEEE (2022)
14. Zhou, S., Alon, U., Agarwal, S., Neubig, G.: CodeBERTScore: evaluating code generation with pretrained models of code (2023). arXiv preprint arXiv:2302.05527
15. Zhang, L., Cao, C., Wang, Z., Liu, P.: Which features are learned by CodeBert: an empirical study of the BERT-based source code representation learning (2023). arXiv preprint arXiv: 2301.08427
16. Das, A.K., Yadav, S., Dhal, S.: Detecting code smells using deep learning. In: TENCON 2019–2019 IEEE Region 10 Conference (TENCON), (pp. 2081–2086). IEEE (2019)
17. Marian, Z., Czibula, I.G., Czibula, G.: A hierarchical clustering-based approach for software restructuring at the package level. In: 2017 19th International Symposium on Symbolic and Numeric Algorithms for Scientific Computing (SYNASC), (pp. 239–246). IEEE (2017)
18. Kaur, I., Kaur, A.: A novel four-way approach designed with ensemble feature selection for code smell detection. IEEE Access **9**, 8695–8707 (2021)

# Next Generation Computing

# Demand-Based Secured Data Transmission in WSN

Prahallad Kumar Sahu[1(✉)], Bhramar Bar Biswal[1], Soumya Ranjan Mishra[1], Jagannath Padhy[2], and Dinesh Kumar[3]

[1] Department CSA, GIET University, Gunupur, Odisha, India
{prahalladsahu,bhramarabarbiswal,soumyaranjanmishra}@giet.edu

[2] Department CSE, Centurian University, Paralakhemundi, Odisha, India
jagannath.padhy20@cutm.ac.in

[3] Department EEE, Centurian University, Paralakhemundi, Odisha, India
dinesh.kumar@cutm.ac.in

**Abstract.** Based on the popularity of the application of wireless sensor networks (WSN) in our day- to-day lives, most of the research is going on in this area. Where data transmission of secure data takes the major role. As the information flow rate in the communication system, the integrity should be maintained. In this paper, we have planned a new approach to send the encrypted data from the Cluster head to the base station using the RSA algorithm. The data are sent to the base station based on the demand generated by the base station. Hence, less amount of energy is consumed by the sensor nodes. This approach is simulated using an NS3 simulator and the result is compared with several algorithms. Based on various parameters our approach takes supremacy over those.

**Keywords:** Cluster head · Non-cluster head · data security · data integrity

## 1 Introduction

Data transmission takes the major role in wireless communication. As the data move freely over the sensor network security is an issue. Many algorithms are developed to transmit the secure data all over the WSN [1]. Only the authentication is given to sender and receiver. They have the access to those data. Te data security mechanism [4] can be implemented as the data masking, data erasure, data encoding and the data backup. Data encoding or data encryption takes the supremacy over these techniques. Where, authentication concept is used. Using this concept, the sender has to use a password, the encryption decryption key, biometric data or some other techniques to verify the correctness of data.

In a cluster [2], generally the cluster head (CH) [3] is responsible for data transmission. The CH is selected among several nodes deployed in the sensor network. Each node is a sensor node and responsible for data sensing and data transmission. A group of sensor nodes based on some constraints, are grouped together to form a cluster. These


R. Kumar et al. (Eds.): ICNGCCA 2025, LNICST 665, pp. 37–44, 2026.
https://doi.org/10.1007/978-3-032-13009-9_4

nodes have the power to select their leader node of the group called as CH. This CH collects data from each of its follower. The follower nodes are called non cluster head (NCH). A variety of cryptography algorithms are proposed for data security. Such as DES/3DES, AES, BLOWFISH, TWOFISH, MD5, HMAC, and RSA etc.

In this Paper, we are using RSA Cryptography algorithm [10] for data encryption. The Rivets-Shamir-Adelman (RSA) algorithm is based on public key concept. For simple distribution of the secret key this concept is used. It assures data integrity and non-repudiation of data. When this concept is used with cluster in wireless transmission it results best in correctness of data. Based on encryption and decryption key[7–9], algorithms are classified into three types. In Secret Key Cryptography (SKC), a single key is used for both encode and decode data. In Public Key Cryptography (PKC), two separate keys are used for encoding and decoding. These are named as public key and private key respectively. In Hash Functions (HF), no key is used, rather a transformation function is used for encryption and decryption.

In this paper, we have proposed a new algorithm to transmit secured data from the cluster head (CH) to the base station (BS). This paper is organized into 5 sections. Section 1 includes the introduction of the concept. In Sect. 2, some of the related papers are reviewed with its pros and area of improvement. Section 3 describes the proposed methods with the associated algorithms. A theoretical example has been taken into consideration to encrypt the wavelength sensed by the sensor node in underwater sensor network (UWSN). Also the decryption at the base station is also discussed over here. In Sect. 4, the simulation result is shown. Section 5 includes the conclusion part of the paper.

## 2 Related Works

Demand based the data transmission techniques [5] is used for reducing the numbers of transmission on data [14]. Demand is generated from the CH and is fulfilled by NCH by sensing the sensed data. Frequency of transmission on data is reduced as well as the energy ingestion. However, raw data is transmitted here without any encryption. A new technique called for data transmission in Multi-hop clustering [6] is proposed for data transmission [12].It is a demand data transmitting algorithm. A new CH is selected each time if it fails some criteria. A supporting cluster head (SCH) is also selected to add fault tolerance to the network. It makes the system fault tolerant but the data security is again an issue.

The data may not be lost over here bur data integrity cannot be assumed. In this proposed method, an energy efficient secure routing for WSN through signal to noise ratio (SNR) (ESRP) [3], clusters, CHs and NCHs are formed based on energy. Malicious nodes are isolated to achieve data security. But more energy is utilized to select the CH and frequent data transmission. In the paper [10] RSA algorithm is implemented to make the data secure.

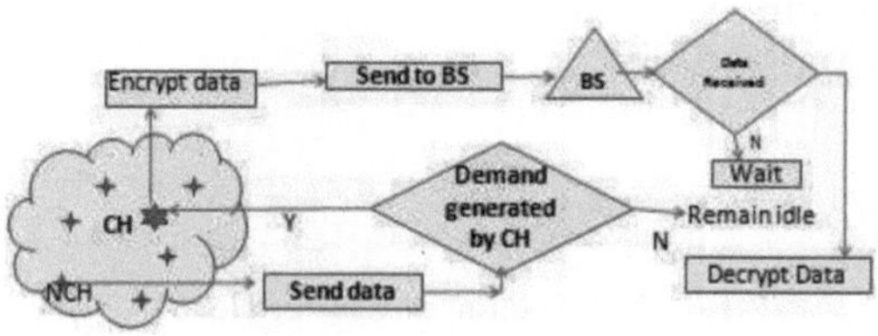


**Figure1: Proposed Model**

**Fig. 1.** Framework of proposed approach

However, where the data encryption is done and where is to be sent is lacked. Its only about the sender and the receiver, but no environment is mentioned here. A modified Stable Election Protocol (SEP) [11], is proposed with random non-uniformed deployments of the node in the network. It uses a mobile sink. It is based on secure data transmission in a best route. In this proposed method, RSA algorithm is used. The method framework is as shown in the Fig. 1. The CH collects the data from its belonging NCHS, process the data as the average value, encrypt the data using RSA algorithm and sent to the base station. The BS obtain the data sent by the CHS and decrypt the value to get the original data. The algorithm describes various steps of data transmission. In Fig. 2 mentioned Algorithm 1 describes the selection of CH in the sensor network. SNR values of each node are stored in a list. The node with the highest SNR value is always extracted to select as the CH if its energy is greater than the pre-assumed threshold energy value. In algorithm 2 (in Fig. 3.), the NCHS selection procedures are described. Euclidean distance between the NCHs and each CHS is computed. The minimum distance and the corresponding CH are assumed to be the leader for the considered NCH. In algorithm 3(in Fig. 4.), the encryption and the decryption process is shown concerning the sensed data, the public key, and the private key.

**Algorithm 1: -**

**Selection of Cluster Head**

1. For j=1 to k
2. Extract ax(SNR[i])
3. If(node[i]. energy> $E_{TH}$)
4. CH[j]=node[i]
5. get node(CH[j])

**Fig. 2.** Selection of Cluster Head

**Algorithm 2: -**

**Selection of Non Cluster Head**

1. For i=1 to n-k
2. cNCH[j]=0 // count of total NCH under jth cluster
3. $mCH[j] = \emptyset$
4. for j= 1 to k
5. $d[i][j] = \sqrt{(x_j - x_i)^2 + (y_j - y_i)^2}$ // distance of ith node from jth cluster
6. $d[i] = ExtractMin(d[i][j])$
7. $mCH[j] = mCH[j] \cup \{node[i]\}$
8. cNCH[j]++

**Fig. 3.** Selection of Non Cluster Head

**Algorithm 3: -**

**Data Encryption**

1. For each CH j =1 to k
2. detaCH[j] = 0
3. For each i=1 to cNCH[j]
4. If(receivedData[i] != 0 )
5. detaCH[j] = detaCH[j] + receivedData[i]
6. FinalDataCH[j] = Avg(DataCH[j])
7. SendDataCH[j] = RSA(FinalDataCH[j],n,e,d) //data encryption
8. Send SendDataCH[j] to BS // at base station as receiver
9. Decrypt data

**Fig. 4.** Data Encryption

**Example:**

**Assumption: -**

i. The standard value of data sensed is 15m
ii. No of NCH in a Cluster 5
iii. Sensed values are 15,15,15,15,16
iv. Prime numbers p and q are 11 3 respectively
v. Encryption key e=3
vi. Decryption key d=7

**Steps:**

1. At CH average value
   v= int (16+16+16+16+16)/4= 16
2. n=p X q=33
3. encrypted data E=$v^3 \; mod \, n$ = $16^3 \; mod \; 33$
   i. = 4
4. decrypted key D=$E^7 \; mod \, n$ = $4^7 \; mod \; 33$ = 16

**Fig. 5.** Data Assumption

## 3 Simulation and Result

This approach is imitative using the NS3 simulator the following results are observed. A grid of 100X100 is deployed with 50 numbers of nodes. The nodes are divided into 6 clusters. According to the parameters listed in Table 1, the following results are obtained. Figure 5. Shows the probability of data loss as compared to the fault tolerance multi-hop (FTMH) with the proposed approach demand based secured data transmission (DBSD). As FTMH takes the help of supporting CH, chances of data lost is less as compared to DBSD. In Fig. 6., we have categorized the measure of data integrity be- tween DBSD and FTMH and DBSD takes the supremacy. The energy utilization [13]is compared be- tween energy efficient secured routing (ESRP) in Fig. 7. Less amount of energy is utilized in the pro- posed approach as it is based on demand concept.

The relative frequency of data transmitting is less in DBSD. In Fig. 8. we have compared the number of times a CH can act as it is when the number of nodes are increasing. Once the number of nodes de- ployed in the network increased, the amount of NCH in a cluster also increase. Hence, the processing time of the CH increased. Thereby, the life time decreases with respect to the increasing time. When its energy become less than the threshold value it can't act as a CH.

**Table 1:** Simulation Parameter

| | |
|---|---|
| Area of sensing field | 100 X 100 |
| Initial energy | 2.4j |
| Number of Clusters | 6 |
| Sensing range | 10m |
| Electronic energy dissipation | 50nj/bit |
| Amplifier energy dissipation | 100pj/bit/m2 |

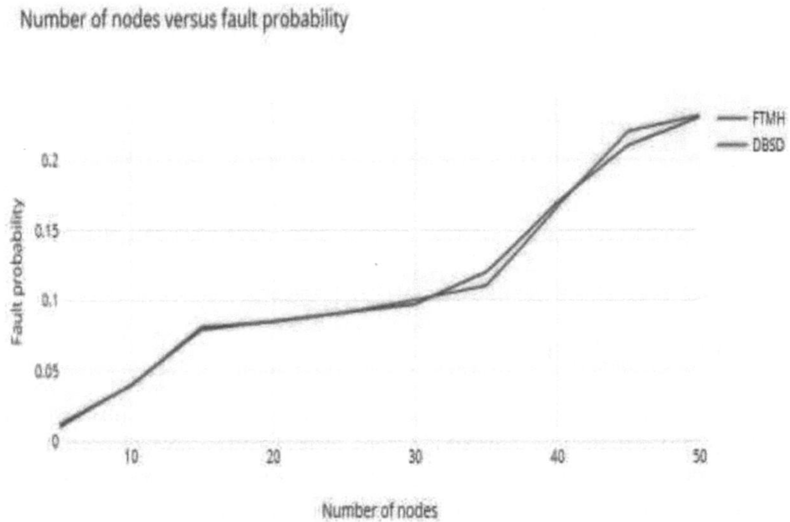


**Fig. 6.** Number of nodes versus fault probability

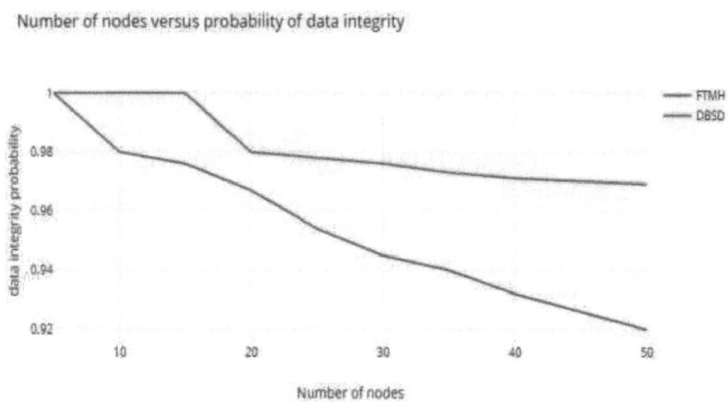


**Fig. 7.** Number of nodes versus probability of data integrity

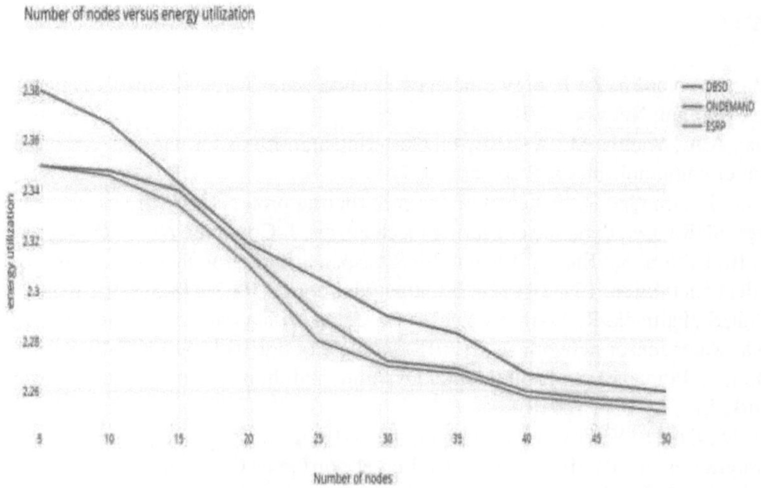


**Fig. 8.** Number of nodes versus energy utilization

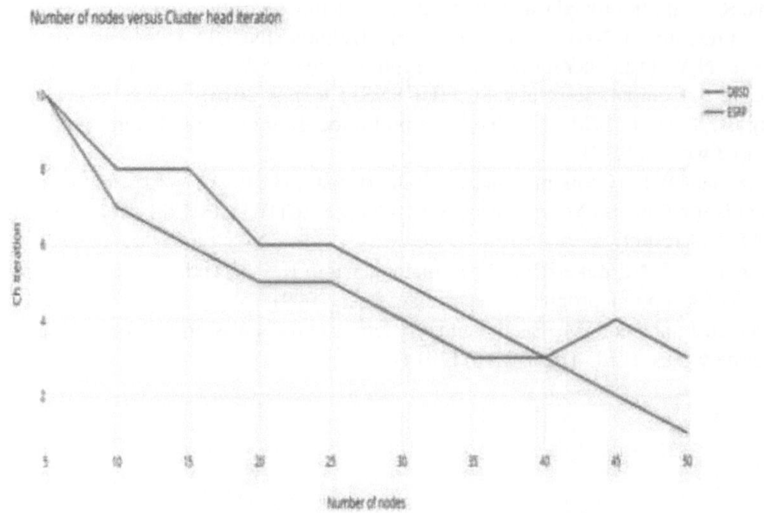


**Fig. 9.** Number of nodes versus CH iteration

## 4 Conclusion

In this paper, we reviewed several issues related to data transmission and data security. A new approach named demand-based secured data transmission (DBSD) is proposed. It works on two steps. In the first steps data is secured by applying the RSA algorithm. And in the second step the data transmission is initiated only after the demand is generated by the base station. As we are transmitting data based on demand, data transmission frequency is reduced. Less amount of energy is consumed by these transmissions. By using this approach data integrity constraint is achieved and energy is also saved. Hence, the network lifetime increases.

## References

1. Ammar, B., Nordin, Z.: Energy efficiency in underwater wireless sensors networks. Energ. Effic. Commun. Netw. **47** (2012)
2. Abbasi, A.A., Younis, M.: A survey on clustering algorithms for wireless sensor net- works- computer communications. Elsevier (2007)
3. Ganesh, S., Amutha, R.: Efficient and secure routing protocol for wireless sensor networks through SNR based dynamic clustering mechanisms. J. Commun. Netw. **15**, 422–429 (2013)
4. Sahu, B., Pabitra, K.: Energy efficient SNR based clustering in underwa- ter sensor network with data encryption. 137–141 (2016). https://doi.org/10.1007/978-3-319-28034-9_18
5. Bandita, S., Pattnaik, R., Dash, P., panda.: On-demand data transmission in multi-hop cluster in underwater sensor network, 1–5 (2018). https://doi.org/10.1109/I2CT.2018.8529743
6. Bandita, S., Prahallad, S.: Fault tolerant Dynamic multihop clustering in under- water sensor network. In: 17th ICIT (2018)
7. Ankit, D., Dhaka, V.: A novel cryptographic and steganographic approach for secure cloud data migration. In: 2015 International Conference on Green Computing and Internet of Things (ICGCIoT). IEEE (2015)
8. Sharma, N., Chirgaiya, S.: A novel approach to hill cipher. Int. J. Comput. Appl. **108**, 34–37 (2014). https://doi.org/10.5120/18958-0285
9. Sapna, R., et al.: Improved way to enhance information security using hybrid cryptography on WSN: a research. J. Netw. Commun. Emerg. Technol. (JNCET) www. jncet. org 7.7 (2017)
10. Goshwe, N.Y.: Data encryption and decryption using RSA algorithm in a network environment. Int. J. Comput. Sci. Netw. Sec. (IJCSNS) **13**(7), 9 (2013)
11. Georgios, S., et al.: SEP: A Stable Election Protocol for clustered hetero- geneous wireless sensor networks (2014)
12. Heinzelman, W.R., Chandrakasan, A., Balakrishnan, H.: Energy –Efficient communication Protocols for Wireless Micro sensor Networks (LEACH). In: HICSS , vol. 8, Maui, Hawaii, p. 30053014 (2000)
13. Halgamuge, M. N., Zukerman M., Ramamohanarao K., Vu, H. L.: An estimation of sensor energy consumption, progress. Electromag. Res. (2009)
14. Lu, H., Li, J., Guizani, M.: Secure and efficient data transmission for cluster- based wireless sensor networks. IEEE Trans. **25**(3) (2014)

# GA-WWO: An Optimised Hybrid Genetic Approach for Scheduling and Balancing Task Loads in Cloud Computing

Nihar Ranjan Sabat[1](✉), Rashmi Ranjan Sahoo[2], Biswaranjan Acharya[3], and Raghvendra Kumar[4]

[1] Faculty of Engineering, Biju Patnaik University of Technology (BPUT), Odisha, Rourkela 769015, India
n.ranjan9@gmail.com

[2] Department of Computer Science and Engineering, Parala Maharaja Engineering College (PMEC), Odisha, Berhampur 761003, India
rashmiranjan.cse@pmec.ac.in

[3] Department of Computer Engineering - AI and Big Data Analytics, Marwadi University, Gujarat, Rajkot 360003, India
biswaacharya@ieee.org

[4] Department of Computer Science and Engineering, GIET University, Gunupur, Odisha 765022, India
raghvendra@giet.edu

**Abstract.** Considering server data is growing exponentially, cloud-based task scheduling and load balancing are essential fields of study. Task scheduling, load balancing are optimized via cloud resource and task monitoring. It is easily adaptable to the complexity and scale of the cloud environment. We propose utilizing a hybrid genetic algorithm that combines genetic algorithm and water wave optimization to coordinate and distribute tasks in the cloud. The best solution from the final population is then used to optimize task scheduling and load balancing approaches. It significantly reduces the inconsistent performance of cloud-based tasks. The experimental simulation result demonstrates that the proposed approach reduces the Make span by 7% to 16%, Transmission Time by 21% to 30%, Average Waiting Time by 5% to 18%, Degree of Imbalance by 62% to 74%, and enhances resource utilization by 2% to 30% on average, in comparison to the PSO, LOA, ACO, Firefly Optimization, SFO and ABC approaches for ten VMs.

**Keywords:** Cloud computing · Genetic Algorithm · Water Wave Optimization · Load balancing · Task scheduling · Virtual machine

## 1 Introduction

Cloud computing technology is being explored as a means to improve the efficiency of industries by utilizing on-premises services. This technology is acquiring and creating insights that add value to product delivery. Bridging the gap between what clients expect


R. Kumar et al. (Eds.): ICNGCCA 2025, LNICST 665, pp. 45–59, 2026.
https://doi.org/10.1007/978-3-032-13009-9_5

and what service providers actually deliver is a further objective of this technique for maintaining customer service [1]. Within the cloud, physical resources are concealed by a layer of virtualization, while acceleration technologies enable programmes to directly interface with the hardware. Cloud-based computing has the potential to address these challenges by providing a cost-effective solution to access specialized acceleration technology using ordinary cloud interfaces [2]. A new computing paradigm, which combines aspects of grid, public, and SaaS, is the result of the emergence of distributed, parallel, along with grid computing. Computing tasks are allocated to computers spread out across the internet instead of local computers or servers in other places with computing in the cloud, which is an important part of this strategy [3]. Cloud based computing provides a web-based, pay-as-you-go services. Service Level Agreements are absolutely essential to Cloud Service Provider-User interactions. This permits providers to be held financially accountable for any expectations that are not achieved [4].

Cloud computing facilitates the efficient and effective development processes of businesses and enables the outsourcing and management of software development across several geographical locations. Organizations and application developers utilize cloud computing to generate high-quality software. The use of the cloud has a significant influence on the artificial complexity that is employed in software development and design. Software development firms utilize it for outsourcing tasks because of its scalability and availability. Developing current software is highly advantageous as it provides a novel approach to creating real-time, cost-effective, and high-quality software. Providers, developers, and consumers are charged based on their utilization of platforms, software, and infrastructure. The widespread usage of cloud-based software applications indicates a rising trend in popularity [5].

In order to accomplish the complexity, dynamic nature, and high-performance requirements associated with modern cloud-based environments, a hybrid task scheduling and load balancing technique needs to be developed. Such an algorithm can significantly enhance performance, resource utilization, energy efficiency, cost-effectiveness, quality of service (QoS), scalability, adaptability, and resilience. Addressing these objectives is critical to sustaining and improving the efficiency, dependability, and sustainability of cloud computing infrastructures. The proposed hybrid algorithm for scheduling tasks & balance of load strategies in cloud-based computing has the potential to make a significant and diverse impact. Here are the main contributions of the algorithm:

- It has the ability to substantially minimize the Make span, Transmission Time, along with Average Waiting Time, hence enhancing the overall performance of the system.
- Optimization of scheduling tasks as well as resource allocation lead to enhanced throughput.
- It enables the most effective utilization of computing resources, prohibiting both underutilization as well as overutilization.
- Tasks can be evenly allocated among the resources that are currently available, so alleviating bottlenecks and maintaining a fair distribution of task load.

In Sect. 2, we take a quick glance at some existing research articles. Section 3 outlines the proposed approach based on a mathematical model. Performance measures are used to compare the efficacy of the proposed and current models, as described in Sect. 4. Section 5 contains a conclusive summary.

## 2 Literature Survey

An efficient scheduling approach optimizes resource utilization as well as minimizes makespan. The task scheduling model, which optimizes scheduling tasks using the golden sine and nonlinear inertia weight coefficient [6]. A novel hybrid optimization algorithm incorporating flower pollination behaviour with the grey wolf optimizer strategy has been proposed to deal with multipurpose task scheduling in diverse IaaS cloud environments, leveraging the evolutionary algorithms crossover operators [7]. A novel approach incorporating three optimization techniques, such as Tabu Search, Bayesian Classification, along with Whale Optimization, has been proposed to reduce Total Execution Cost as well as Total Execution Time while mapping [8]. It compares cloud scheduling to natural selection, which describes biological evolution. A way to solve problems faster is by offering the optimal answer. It enables versatility, parallel processing, and global optimization. The cost function also chooses the best option based on operational completion time, resource pricing, and load balancing [9]. The MOMFO algorithm improves fog cloud computing based IoT services by reducing the completion of tasks, system throughput, and energy consumption. Lowering energy use reduces CO2 emissions. Datasets are used to evaluate the scheduling of tasks [10]. The incorporation of the grey wolf optimization method and the genetic algorithm reduces the time, energy, and cost of multi-objective scheduling of tasks. Using the genetic algorithms crossover and mutation operators enhances the algorithm [11]. A novel hybrid scheduling of tasks strategy makes use of ant colony optimization to develop initial pheromone dispersal following particle swarm optimization that quickly determines the initial solution [12]. An advanced genetic load-balancing approach for hybrid clouds has been proposed. A genetic algorithm (GA) addresses hybrid cloud load balancing issues, whereas a Gated Recurrent Unit (GRU) model classifies and prioritizes virtual machines. TensorFlow assessed the cloud environment and load balancer [13].

The most common ways of organizing tasks and distributing tasks in cloud computing have some flaws. Predetermined resource allocation and inflexibility limit some techniques. Heuristic techniques often become trapped in local optima, miss the global optimal solution, and need help adapting to shifting cloud environments. Most load balancing systems only intervene when performance declines, causing inefficiencies and service delays. In addition, they often priorities response time over energy usage, cost, and service level agreements. Metaheuristic algorithms that converge prematurely to inferior solutions and lack scalability may be inefficient in large, complex cloud systems. The diversity of cloud resources, which range in performance, cost, and availability, as well as the extremely changeable and uncertain nature of cloud-based tasks, are typically difficult for existing methods to manage.

A hybrid approach effectively manages the trade-off between exploration and exploitation, through using an amalgamation of search techniques that diversify as well as adapt to real-time changes. It also monitors cloud resources and tasks, optimizes task scheduling and load balancing, optimizes utilization of resources, reduces waste, and streamlines the distribution of loads. It is adaptable to the complexity and magnitude of the cloud environment.

This paper presents a novel approach that combines genetic algorithms and water wave optimization. It takes advantage of genetic algorithms' global search features and water wave optimization's local search effectiveness while resulting in an excellent solution for scheduling tasks and load balancing in dynamic cloud environments. By ensuring a balance between exploration and exploitation, this hybrid strategy enhances performance levels overall.

# 3 Proposed Methodology

Cloud computing concerns with resource sharing, scheduling tasks, and balancing load as demand for services continue to rise. Consequently, several heuristic and metaheuristic algorithms have been developed in an effort to enhance performance. By combining search methods that diversify and respond to real-time changes, hybrid approaches balance exploration with exploitation. Monitoring cloud resources and tasks optimizes task scheduling, load balancing, and load distribution. It can readily adapt to the complexity and magnitude of the cloud environment. This research introduces a fresh approach which incorporates genetic algorithms with water wave optimization. This section includes a discussion of the proposed algorithms.

Based on Darwin's concept of natural selection, genetic algorithms choose the fittest for the upcoming generation. They are especially beneficial for problems in which the search space is big, complicated, or poorly understood [14]. Water wave optimization is a nature-inspired method that models how water waves propagate and refract in the natural world. This algorithm is based on the phenomenon of water waves spreading out, breaking, and refocusing when they hit various terrains or impediments [15].

Genetic algorithms are adept in navigating an array of possibilities through processes such as crossover and mutation, whereas Water Wave Optimization exhibits the solution refinement by analyzing wave phenomena such as refraction and breaking, thereby facilitating convergence to optimal outcomes. WWO's wave dynamics enable rapid adaptation to fluctuations in cloud environments, such as changing tasks or resource availability, while GA's evolutionary approaches enhance this adaptability, enabling the system to respond effectively to dynamic conditions. In order to reduce the likelihood of encountering local optima, a hybrid approach balances global search, which involves exploration, with local optimization, which involves refinement. The amalgamation of GA's diversification with WWO's intensification expedites the development of effective solutions. Efficient resource distribution reduces operational expenses and reduces waste. Effective task allocation improves processing rates and maintains performance as the system expands. The hybrid approach ensures consistent performance across fluctuating tasks.

## 3.1 Problem Definition for Task Scheduling and Load Balancing

To optimize task scheduling and load balancing in a dynamic cloud environment, the problem has been stated, the optimization technique has been developed, and the integration of both algorithms into a mathematical model has been described. The following is a methodical approach.

Cloud computing necessitates the execution of numerous tasks to optimize the utilization of cloud technology. These tasks are essential for achieving maximum flexibility, scalability, cost-effectiveness, and denoted by $T = \{T_1, T_2, ..., T_n\}$.

Cloud computing entails handling the operation of resources, for example storage, computation, and network services. These resources are designed to clarify cloud-based task scheduling and load balancing. Some significant resources and strategies in cloud computing for task scheduling and load balancing are denoted by $R = \{R_1, R_2, ..., R_m\}$. In cloud-based scenarios, R encompasses a wide range of resources, each of which serves a particular purpose. This research is aimed to maximize resource use, minimize makespan, transmission time, waiting time, degree of imbalance.

To optimize resource utilization, minimize makespan, transmission time, waiting time, and imbalance in cloud computing, these objectives are incorporated into a single formulation. To facilitate the integration of each component into a holistic fitness function, the following is a detailed breakdown:

Resource Utilization (RU) is the ratio of used resources to the total available resources, mathematically denoted by Eq. (1).

$$RU = \frac{ResourcesUsed}{ResourcesAvailable} \tag{1}$$

Total time required to execute a set of tasks is known as Makespan (M) formally illustrated in Eq. (2).

$$M = Max\big(T_{Completion}(i)\big) \tag{2}$$

where $T_{Completion}(i)$ represents the completion time of task i.

Transmission Time (TT) is the total length of time needed for transmitting data among nodes, represented by Eq. (3).

$$TT = \sum\nolimits_{i=1}^{n} T_{Transmission}(i) \tag{3}$$

where $T_{Transmission}(i)$ stands for the transmission time for task i.

Waiting Time (WT) is the aggregate amount of time that tasks remain in the queue prior to execution, as demonstrated in Eq. (4).

$$WT = \sum\nolimits_{i=1}^{n} T_{Waiting}(i) \tag{4}$$

where $T_{Waiting}(i)$ denotes the waiting time for task i.

In terms of Eq. (5), the Degree of Imbalance (DI) is a measure of a fair distribution of tasks among the resources available.

$$DI = \frac{Max(RU_i) - Min(RU_i)}{\sum_{i=1}^{m} RU_i} \tag{5}$$

where the parameter $RU_i$ represents the resource utilization of resource i, while m represents the total number of resources.

In order to incorporate all of the objectives into a Final Fitness Function (F), a weighted sum approach has been used, with each objective multiplied by a weight according to its computational significance, as expressed in Eq. (6).

$$F = w_1 \cdot RU - w_2 \cdot \frac{1}{M} - w_3 \cdot \frac{1}{TT} - w_4 \cdot \frac{1}{WT} - w_5 \cdot \frac{1}{DI} \tag{6}$$

*The weights allocated to every objective are denoted by* $w_1$, $w_2$, $w_3$, $w_4$ *and* $w_5$.*The RU should be maximised, hence it should be added right then. To reduce M, TT, WT, and DI, their reciprocals are used to convert minimization objectives into maximization terms, or they are subtracted outright. By adjusting the weights* $w_1$, $w_2$, $w_3$, $w_4$ *and* $w_5$*, it is possible to prioritise various aspects of the optimisation based on the cloud computing environment's specific requirements.*

## 3.2 Stages of Operation

Incorporating Genetic Algorithm (GA) with Water Wave Optimisation (WWO) can make task scheduling and load balancing more effective in an evolving cloud realm by using the strongest parts of both. The optimisation method will be defined, and the combined effect of both approaches will be discussed. Here's an organised approach:

### 3.2.1 Stages of Genetic Algorithm (GA)

i. *Initialization*: Set the initial P solutions, each x representing a task schedule, randomly.
ii. *Selection*: Choose parents according to their level of fitness.
iii. *Crossover*: Combine elements of two parent solutions to create offspring.
iv. *Mutation*: Switch the locations of two tasks in a schedule to add variation.
v. *Fitness Evaluation*: Consider each solution x in the population and assess its fitness f(x).

### 3.2.2 Stages of Water Wave Optimization (WWO)

*i. Wave Propagation*

The position of each wave that represents a solution is updated according to Eq. (7)

$$X_i^{t+1} = X_i^t + \lambda \cdot r \cdot (U - L) \tag{7}$$

*A random vector is represented by r, U and L are the upper and lower limits of the search space, and* $\lambda$ *is a decreasing function.*

*ii. Wave Refraction*

The wave's direction changes according to the best solution described in Eq. (8)

$$X_i^{t+1} = X_i^t + \gamma \cdot \left(X_{best} - X_i^t\right) \tag{8}$$

$\gamma$ *indicates the refraction coefficient, whilst* $X_{best}$ *is the optimal solution noticed so far.*

*iii. Wave Breaking*

Subsequent solutions have been generated from a past solution in accordance with a specified criterion that initiates their development, as demonstrated by Eq. (9).

$$X_j^{t+1} = X_i^t + \delta \cdot r \cdot (U - L) \tag{9}$$

The symbol $\delta$ represents the breaking coefficient.

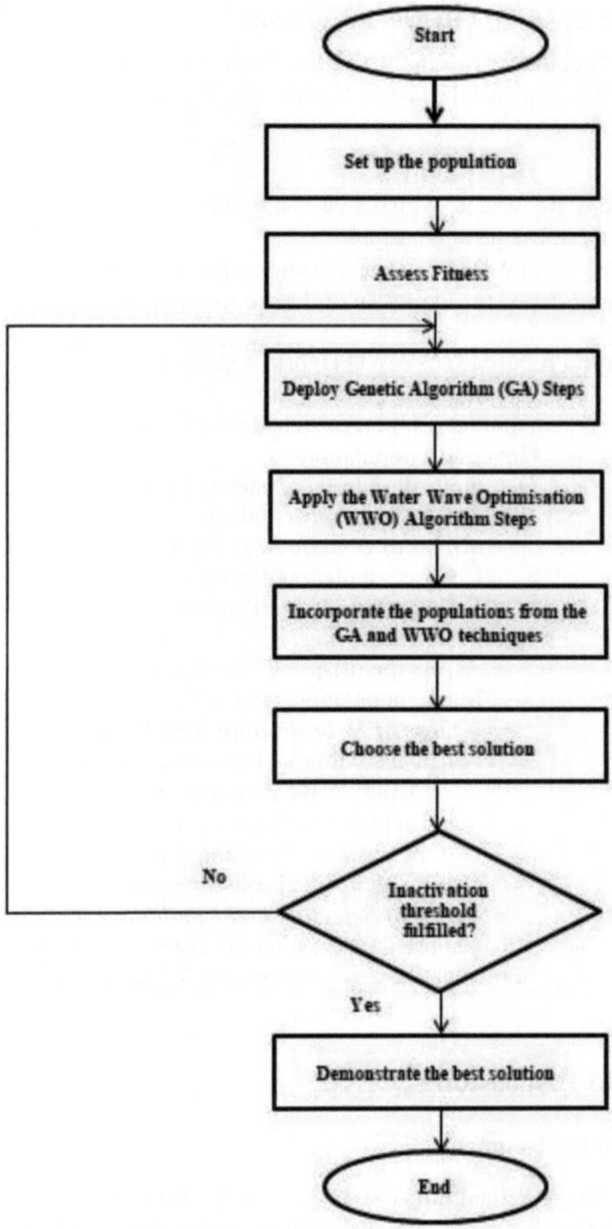


**Fig. 1.** Workflow of the proposed model

### 3.2.3 Stages of GA-WWO Hybrid Integration

Incorporation of populations from the Genetic Algorithm (GA) along with Water Wave Optimization (WWO) phases has been described by Eq. (10).

$$P_{Combined} = P_{GA} \cup P_{WWO} \tag{10}$$

i, New populations are created, with the best solutions from $P_{Combined}$ chosen based on their fitness for the subsequent iterations.

ii. Phases of GA and WWO are repeated until a threshold or convergence is attained. Figure 1 demonstrates the workflow of the proposed model.

| **Algorithm**: Proposed GA-WWO Hybrid Algorithm | |
|---|---|
| **Input:** | Population $P_k$ , $1 \le k \le n$ |
| **Output:** | Optimal solution for scheduling tasks & balancing loads |
| 1: | Generate a population |
| 2: | Determine the fitness of each solution across the population |
| 3: | While stopping criterion failed |
| 4: | ***//Steps of Genetic Algorithm*** |
| 5: | Choose population parents |
| 6: | Create offspring with crossover |
| 7: | Mutate offspring |
| 8: | Assess the offspring's fitness |
| 9: | Merge populations with offspring |
| 10: | ***// Steps of Hybridization with WWO*** |
| 11: | For each solution in the merged population |
| 12: | Deploy wave propagation |
| 13: | Employ wave refraction |
| 14: | Allow wave breaking if required |
| 15: | Determine updated solution's fitness |
| 16: | ***// Step of Selection and Combination*** |
| 17: | Choose the best solution to develop a new population |
| 18: | Implement best task scheduling & load balancing solution |

# 4 Result and Discussion

## 4.1 Simulation Environment

This research leverages CloudSim v6.0.0-beta, an effective and scalable simulation tool, to explore resource allocation, task distribution, and optimization strategies inside a regulated virtualized system. The simulation has been carried out on a conventional desktop computer equipped with an Intel Core processor. The Intel i7 processor can run multi-threaded processes; the system has 16 GB of RAM, allocating 12 GB for the simulation environment, 4 GB for the operating system, along with a 1 TB hard drive for the simulation framework and data operations. Table 1 illustrates the parameters of the simulation environment necessary for the proposed research.

**Table 1.** Parameters of Simulation

| Parameter | Specification |
|---|---|
| **Host Machine Specifications** | |
| Processor | Intel Core i7 |
| RAM | 16 GB |
| Hard Disk | 1 TB |
| Operating System | Windows 10 Enterprise |
| RAM Allocated to OS | 4 GB |
| **Simulation Environment** | |
| Number of Datacenters | 1 |
| Number of Hosts | 10 |
| Host Memory Size | 2 GB per host |
| Host Storage Capacity | 100 GB per host |
| Host Bandwidth | 1.5 Gbps per host |
| Number of VMs per Host | 6 |
| **Virtual Machine Specifications** | |
| Total Number of VMs | 10 |
| MIPS per VM | 1,000 |
| Image Size | 50 GB per VM |
| Memory Size | 512 MB per VM |
| Bandwidth | 100 Mbps per VM |
| Number of Processing Elements (PEs) | 4 per VM |

## 4.2 Analysis of Results and Discussion

Wide research leveraging genetic algorithms for task scheduling and water wave optimization for localized refinement to reduce data transfer, node transmission delays, and network fatigue. Genetic algorithm resource allocation patterns and water wave optimization gap-filling adaptations optimized scheduling and efficacy. Genetic algorithm water wave optimization synergy and parallelism reduce task completion time, speeding convergence.

Realistic cloud computing enhances transmission time, resource utilization, makespan, average waiting time, and imbalance. E-commerce systems optimize transaction speeds, real-time inventory updates, waiting times, and resource utilization for large volumes and peak shopping periods. Healthcare and telemedicine reduce wait times by processing patient data, including real-time monitoring and diagnostics. Reduced makespan and increased resource utilization speed up data-intensive machine learning training and model iterations. Average waiting times speed task commencement, essential for iterative model construction. The cost-effective, resource-sustainable, user-experience, dependability, scalability, and turnaround time of GA-WWO hybrid approach optimize real-time analytics entities.

The task allocation method in virtual machines (VMs) has been efficiently implemented. Ten virtual machines with different tasks were selected. Quality of service parameters include transmission time, resource utilization, make span, average waiting time, and degree of imbalance. These need to be analyzed during performance analysis. These essential performance parameters were evaluated utilizing a variety of tests involving diverse tasks. An experimental simulation evaluated the proposed GA-WWO Hybrid approach's five quality of service metrics to PSO, LOA, ACO, Firefly Optimization, SFO and ABC for 10 virtual machines.

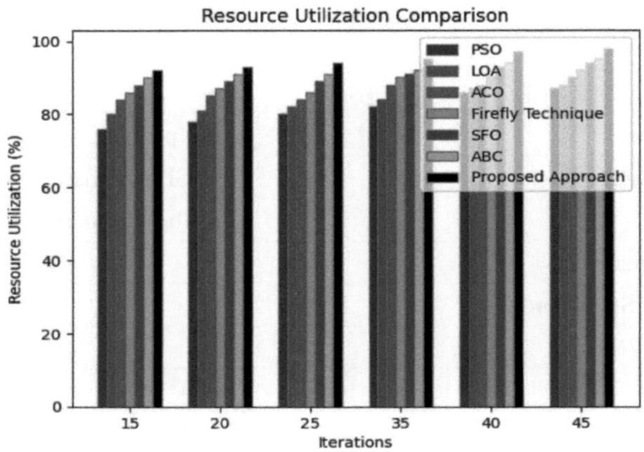


**Fig. 2.** Resource Utilization comparison with varying number of Tasks

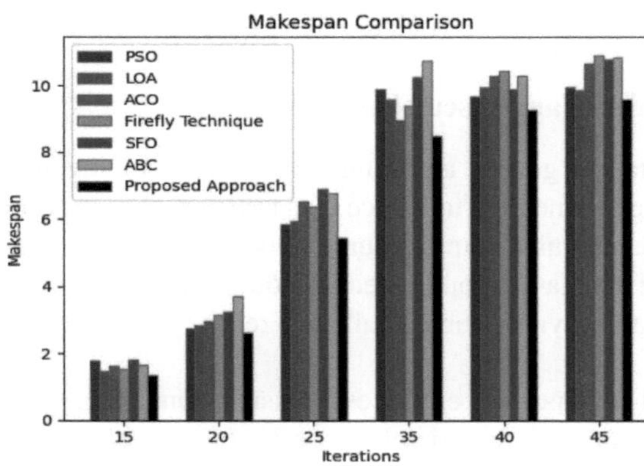


**Fig. 3.** Makespan comparison in relation to varying number of Tasks

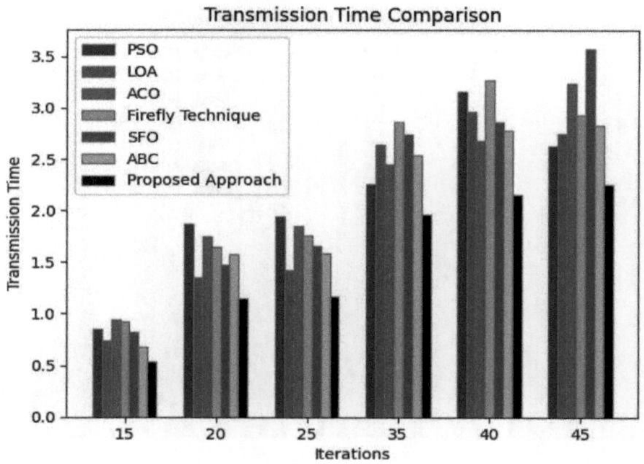


**Fig. 4.** Transmission Time comparison for varying number of Tasks

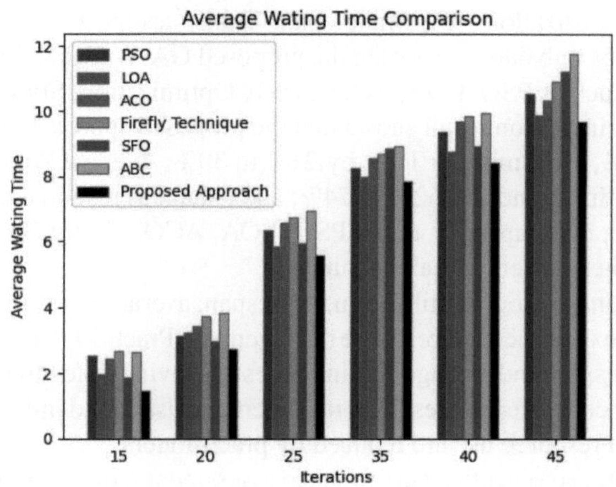


**Fig. 5.** Average Waiting Time at different Task Counts

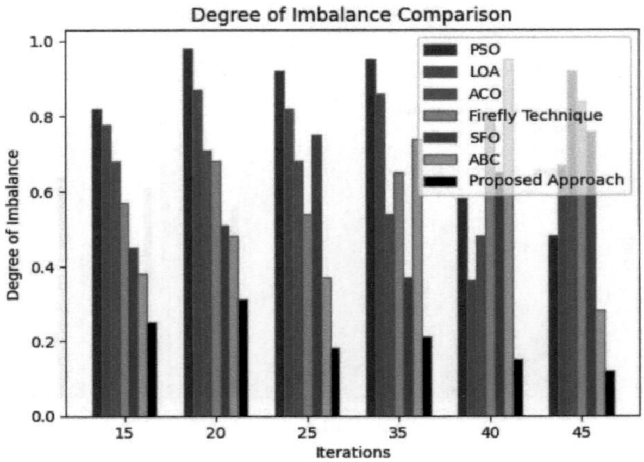


**Fig. 6.** Analyzing the Degree of Imbalance with Varying Numbers of Tasks

Figures 2–6 illustrate a comparison of five important quality of service metrics, namely Resource Utilization (%), Make span, Transmission Time, Average Waiting Time, and Degree of Imbalance, between the proposed GA-WWO Hybrid approach and other approaches such as PSO, LOA, ACO, Firefly Optimization, SFO, as well as ABC. The experimental simulation result shows that the proposed approach reduces the Make span by 7% to 16%, Transmission Time by 21% to 30%, Average Waiting Time by 5% to 18%, Degree of Imbalance by 62% to 74%, and enhances resource utilization by 2% to 30% on average, in comparison to the PSO, LOA, ACO, Firefly Optimization, SFO, and ABC approaches for ten virtual machines.

Transmission time, resource utilization, makespan, average waiting time, and imbalance improve user experience and resource management. Practitioners must reduce transmission time, makespan, and average waiting times to provide faster and more responsive cloud services. For cost-effective resource management, usage and imbalance are crucial. Energy, waste, and resource use are reduced by practitioners.

A rigorous, fair, and objective performance assessment requires a one-way ANOVA to compare Makespan between the suggested strategy and PSO, LOA, ACO, Firefly, SFO, and ABC. This suggested approach's efficiency or effectiveness in task scheduling or optimization can be statistically proven. The Makespan of this method is compared to PSO, LOA, ACO, Firefly Technique, SFO, and ABC. There are six iterations for each algorithm in this comparison. The null hypothesis for this analysis is H0: The seven techniques, including the proposed one, have equal Makespan. H1, the alternative hypothesis, is: The Makespan of the approaches discussed above is unequal. Table 2 summarizes the outcomes of the one-way analysis of variance assessment.

**Table 2.** Findings of the One-Way Analysis of Variance (ANOVA) Test

| | SS | df | MS | F | P |
|---|---|---|---|---|---|
| Between: | 5.782 | 6 | 0.964 | 0.080 | 0.998 |
| Within: | 422.699 | 35 | 12.077 | | |
| Total: | 428.481 | 41 | | | |

The estimated F statistic of.080 is much less than the reported P statistic of.998 in Table 2. The null hypothesis that the mean Makespan of all seven approaches, including the new one, is equal has been rejected, showing that they differ.

One-tailed dependent t-test is useful for pairwise comparisons between the suggested strategy and PSO, LOA, ACO, Firefly, SFO, and ABC, especially when evaluating a specified statistical hypothesis like shorter makespan. This study explored seven approaches, incorporating the paired parametric t-test approach. A total of six paired t-test assessments have been performed to determine the most effective Makespan technique. The proposed approach was compared against PSO, LOA, ACO, Firefly Technique, SFO, and ABC to determine its efficacy. A one-tailed hypothesis test has been carried out with a.05 level of significance. A sample size of $N = 6$ for each test immediately established the degrees of freedom, 6–1, that is 5. Each analytical approach undergoes six iterations to calculate the paired T-test. The null hypothesis states that the proposed approach has the same makespan as the existing approaches. Alternative hypothesis claims that the Makespan of the proposed approach is less than that of the existing approaches currently being assessed. Table 3 illustrates the findings of the paired one-tailed t-test with degrees of freedom $df = (6–1) = 5$, and population mean $\mu = 0$.

**Table 3.** Paired one-tailed t-test Assessment for Two Dependent Means

| Test | Treatment1 | Treatment2 | t | p |
|---|---|---|---|---|
| 1 | PSO | Proposed Work | -2.93 | .01625 |
| 2 | LOA | Proposed Work | -3.27 | .01108 |
| 3 | ACO | Proposed Work | -4.46 | .00333 |
| 4 | Firefly Technique | Proposed Work | -4.79 | .00246 |
| 5 | SFO | Proposed Work | -4.76 | .00252 |
| 6 | ABC | Proposed Work | -4.7 | .00267 |

Table 3 illustrates six tests with p-values < 0.05. So, the null hypothesis is rejected and the alternative hypothesis is accepted, meaning that the proposed approach always has the shortest Makespan.

## 5 Conclusion

Due to exponential server data growth, cloud-based task scheduling and load balancing are critical. Optimization of task scheduling and balanced load is possible by dealing with the complexity along with scale of the cloud-based system. This novel approach incorporates genetic algorithms with water wave optimization to schedule and allocate cloud tasks, simulated in the CloudSim v6.0.0-beta environment. The suggested strategy reduces the Make span by 7% to 16%, Transmission Time by 21% to 30%, Average Waiting Time by 5% to 18%, Degree of Imbalance by 62% to 74%, and enhances resource utilization by 2% to 30% on average, in comparison to the PSO, LOA, ACO, Firefly Optimization, SFO, and ABC approaches across ten virtual machines, as illustrated by the experimental simulation findings.

Scalability of the proposed GA-WWO approach can be assessed by deploying more Virtual Machines (VMs). With more virtual machines, the suggested GA-WWO technique can be used in parallel to lower processing overhead. Improving the proposed approach allows for larger datasets and VM configurations without wasting resources. An increased number of virtual machines may generate a variety of realistic duties, such as variations in task arrival rates, durations, and resource requirements. CPU intensive processes, such as cryptographic computations or matrix operations, are able to model by specifying high MIPS (Million Instructions per Second) requirements in Cloudlet objects. Significant RAM allocation requirements can be established for Cloudlets to emulate memory-intensive task loads, such as massive data processing or in-memory databases.

For SLA compliance, the GA-WWO hybrid approach optimizes task scheduling and transmission times to reduce provider costs and fulfill demand for task processing resources. Cloud providers can deliver more tasks faster and enhance service throughput with shorter makespan. Its hybrid and multi-cloud performance may illustrate its versatility and efficacy in intricate situations involving many resources. Analyzing its interactions with Serverless architectures, edge computing, and decentralized cloud frameworks can clarify its adaptability. This approach can be assessed on AWS, Azure, or Google Cloud with industry cloud providers to identify practical issues and developmental opportunities.

## References

1. Aravinth, S.S., Krishnan, A.S.R., Ranganathan, R., Sasikala, M., Kumar, M.S., Thiyagarajan, R.: Cloud computing—everything as a cloud service in industry 4.0. In: Digital Transformation: Industry 4.0 to Society 5.0, (pp. 103–121). Singapore: Springer Nature Singapore (2024)
2. Rosa, L., Foschini, L., Corradi, A.: Empowering cloud computing with network acceleration: a survey. IEEE Commun. Surv. Tutor. (2024)
3. Abdi, A., Zeebaree, S.R.: Embracing distributed systems for efficient cloud resource management: a review of techniques and methodologies. Indonesian J. Comput. Sci. **13**(2), (2024)
4. Qazi, F., Kwak, D., Khan, F.G., Ali, F., Khan, S.U.: Service level agreement in cloud computing: taxonomy, prospects, and challenges. Int. Things, 101126 (2024)

5. Khan, H.U., Ali, F., Nazir, S.: Systematic analysis of software development in cloud computing perceptions. J. Softw. Evolut. Proc. **36**(2), e2485 (2024)
6. Gong, R., Li, D., Hong, L., Xie, N.: Task scheduling in cloud computing environment based on enhanced marine predator algorithm. Clust. Comput. **27**(1), 1109–1123 (2024)
7. Malti, A.N., Hakem, M., Benmammar, B.: A new hybrid multi-objective optimization algorithm for task scheduling in cloud systems. Clust. Comput. **27**(3), 2525–2548 (2024)
8. Sandhu, R., Faiz, M., Kaur, H., Srivastava, A., Narayan, V.: Enhancement in performance of cloud computing task scheduling using optimization strategies. Cluster Comput. ,1–24 (2024)
9. Alla, V.R.S.P., et al.: Optimizing task scheduling in cloud computing: a hybrid artificial intelligence approach. Cogent Eng. **11**(1), 2328355 (2024)
10. Salehnia, T., et al.: An optimal task scheduling method in IoT-Fog-Cloud network using multi-objective moth-flame algorithm. Multimedia Tools Appl. **83**(12), 34351–34372 (2024)
11. Behera, I., Sobhanayak, S.: Task scheduling optimization in heterogeneous cloud computing environments: a hybrid GA-GWO approach. J. Parallel Distrib. Comput. **183**, 104766 (2024)
12. Sabat, N.R., Sahoo, R.R., Pradhan, M.R., Acharya, B.: Hybrid technique for optimal task scheduling in cloud computing environments. TELKOMNIKA (Telecomm. Comput. Electron. Control) **22**(2), 380–392 (2024)
13. Sabat, N.R., Sahoo, R.R.: Virtual IGA-GRU an approach for load balancing in cloud computing. In: Computing, Communication and Intelligence (1st ed.), pp.71–75, (2025)
14. Qian, L.I., Xue, W.A.N.G.: Modified artificial bee colony algorithm for load balancing in cloud computing environments. Int. J. Adv. Comput. Sci. Applications, 15(5), (2024)
15. Arulkumar, V. and Bhalaji, N. Load balancing in cloud computing using water wave algorithm. Concur. Comput.-Pract. Exper. **34**(8) (2022)

# Big Data Analytics

# A CNN Based Intelligent System For Detection of Tessellated Fundus Images

Bethi Meghana(✉), Kachi Anvesh, Peruri Sireesha,
Maneesh Reddy Devireddy, and Swati Singh

Department of Information Technology, Vardhaman College of Engineering,
Telangana 501218, India
{bethimeghana21it,perurisireesha21it,
maneeshreddydevireddy21it}@student.vardhaman.org

**Abstract.** Our research tackles the problem of identifying fundus tessellation.We diagnose tessellation for a given retinal image using deep learning algorithms on image data. Tessellation is an eye ailment similar to myopia. For the provided image data, we created a CNN-based system to categorize and recognize tessellated fundus patterns. In order to guarantee noise reduction and data augmentation, the image data is first preprocessed using a normalization technique.A CNN model that has several convolutional and pooling layers is then trained using the normalized dataset in order to extract hierarchical features from the pictures. The last layer used to categorize the degree of tessellation is logistic regression.Metrics including area under the curve (AUC), accuracy, and F1 score are used to assess the performance of the model.

**Keywords:** Fundus Tessellation · Machine Learning · Matplotlib Algorithm · Image Processing · Retinal Diseases · Early Diagnosis

## 1 Introduction

Fundus tessellation, a visible pattern on the retina that is a key marker of extreme and pathologic myopia, is often associated with the eye condition known as myopia. Identification of tessellation is essential for early intervention, but the use of conventional treatments is often restricted by manual analysis, which is laborious and imprecise.We created a CNN-based method to identify tessellation in retinal images in order to increase effectiveness and precision.

By employing edge detection, segmentation, and image preprocessing to identify and categorize tessellated patterns, our method assists medical professionals in diagnosing and treating retinal pictures.With this easy-to-use web platform, medical professionals can evaluate and learn from retinal images that seamlessly integrate with clinical operations. [Fig. 1] depicts the structure of tessellated fundus


R. Kumar et al. (Eds.): ICNGCCA 2025, LNICST 665, pp. 63–74, 2026.
https://doi.org/10.1007/978-3-032-13009-9_6

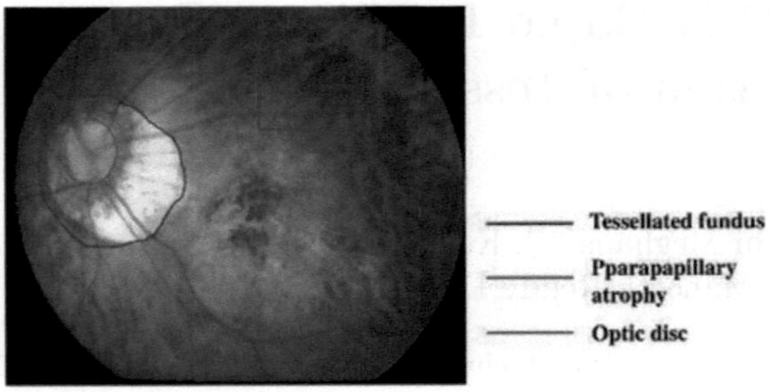


**Fig. 1.** Structure of Tessellated Fundus

## 2 Related Work

Research on the diagnosis and identification of retinal abnormalities has made substantial use of a range of image processing and machine learning techniques. Earlier systems mostly used conventional image processing techniques such histogram equalization and morphological methods to improve and segment retinal pictures. Despite their usefulness, these techniques typically have trouble with variations in image quality and detecting minor clinical characteristics.

In a study by Li et al. [1], the quantitative evaluation of fundus tessellated density in young individuals with various refractive situations using artificial intelligence (AI) is examined. This study assesses how well AI algorithms analyse fundus images from people with different refractive problems using ophthalmic research approaches. Huang et al. [2] demonstrated the potential advantages of prompt diagnosis in younger groups by using AI to screen Chinese youngsters for fundus tessellation. Shao and colleagues [3] demonstrated the use of artificial intelligence in ocular research by evaluating the degree of fundus tessellation using machine learning-based techniques. Similar to this, Wang and associates [4] demonstrated that deep learning works well for identifying myopic maculopathy, a condition that is strongly associated with fundus tessellation.

Retinal vein occlusion (RVO) and age-related macular degeneration (AMD) are two retinal disorders that have received more research attention than tessellated fundus detection. Methods used in these circumstances, however, provide a basis for tessellation study today. Tan et al. [5] employed deep learning to separate retinal layers and detect problems in optical coherence tomography (OCT) images, demonstrating the potential for comparable techniques in identifying tessellated fundus patterns

The analysis of retinal pictures has demonstrated great potential with deep learning, particularly with Convolutional Neural Networks (CNNs). The results of Lyu et al. [6]have been corroborated by research by Wang et al. and Wu et al. [7], which shows that CNNs are successful at identifying tessellated patterns in retinal pictures. According to these findings, CNNs are increasingly being used to analyze medical images.

He et al. [8] clarified the link between tessellation and myopic diseases by examining the density of fundus tessellation in pathological myopia. In parallel, Liu et al. [9]introduced a unique machine learning approach that uses deep learning techniques to automate fundus tessellation identification and quantitative analysis.

Zhang et al. and Liu et al. [12]. broadened the application of AI in detecting tessellated fundus by employing CNNs for automatic identification and mapping the progression of the disease. Their findings show that CNNs can be used to A CNN Based Intelligent System for Detection of Tessellation in Fundus Images 3 address a wide range of retinal conditions.

## 3 Materials and Methodology

### 3.1 Data Collection and Preprocessing

The dataset comprises 12,500 high-resolution retinal images in PNG format, obtained from 200 patients. To guarantee accurate diagnostic insights, each image has been meticulously annotated by experienced ophthalmologists, who indicated the presence or absence of tessellation. This thorough labeling process [10] creates a dataset that is high-quality, clinically significant, and dependable for medical assessments.

In preparation for use with a Convolutional Neural Network (CNN), the images were resized to 224x224 pixels. Various preprocessing techniques [Fig. 3] were employed to improve image quality, methods for reducing noise helped standardize lighting and eliminate unnecessary details that could obscure vital features. Furthermore, converting to grayscale and applying edge detection [Fig. 2.] enhanced the clarity of retinal patterns, facilitating segmentation and highlighting important regions critical for precise diagnostics [11].

### 3.2 Image Augmentation and Normalization

Data augmentation was carried out using TensorFlow's Image Data Generator to guarantee robustness and model generalization. The augmentation techniques included random rotations (up to 20°C), shifts (up to 20% of image dimensions, zoom up to 20%) , and horizontal flipping.

In addition to improving dataset variety, these techniques assisted in avoiding over fitting. To standardize input data and speed up neural network convergence, pixel intensities were normalized to a range of [0, 1].

### 3.3 Dataset Splitting and Configuration

The dataset was divided into training, validation, and test sets using stratified sampling to preserve the original label distribution across subsets. This split ensured each subset accurately represented the dataset's class distribution, minimizing potential biases and improving model evaluation reliability. Data generators were configured to manage batch processing efficiently for each subgroup, optimizing memory usage during model training [14].

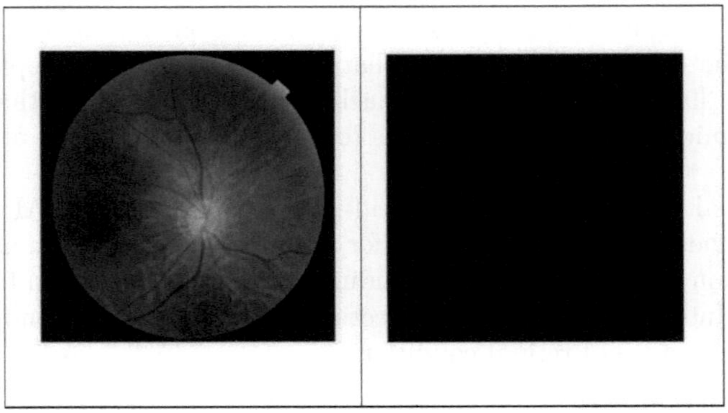

**Fig. 2.** Grayscale Image and Edge detection Image of Fundus figure

### 3.4 Class Imbalance Handling

To solve the class imbalance in the dataset, we adjusted the class weights at the time of model training. This enhanced the model's capacity to detect tessellated patterns, which were less common in the data, by concentrating more on the minority class. We also investigated oversampling the underrepresented class to further balance the data and prevent the model from favoring the dominant class.

### 3.5 Training and Evaluation

After the CNN model was trained across several epochs, some of the data was set aside for validation to monitor model performance and avoid overfitting. We selected a batch size that balances computational efficiency and training stability. After the model was trained on a new test set, key metrics such as recall, accuracy, F1 score, and precision were computed to accurately assess its efficacy. To monitor learning progress and model stability, accuracy and loss curves were displayed for both training and validation sets.

**Segmentation:** The images were initially converted to greyscale[Fig. 4.] to streamline the data and emphasize intensity values over colors, which helps locate important details.

For homogeneity and to lessen the processing load during analysis, the photos were scaled to 224 × 224 pixels. Subsequently, the pixel values were normalized to a range of 0 to 1, which speeds up neural network convergence. Moreover, noise reduction methods such as Gaussian blurring were used to eliminate any anomalies that would prevent precise segmentation.

Test Accuracy: 91.72%

**Model: "sequential_2"**

| Layer (type) | Output Shape | Param # |
|---|---|---|
| conv2d_6 (Conv2D) | (None, 222, 222, 32) | 896 |
| max_pooling2d_6 (MaxPooling2D) | (None, 111, 111, 32) | 0 |
| conv2d_7 (Conv2D) | (None, 109, 109, 64) | 18,496 |
| max_pooling2d_7 (MaxPooling2D) | (None, 54, 54, 64) | 0 |
| conv2d_8 (Conv2D) | (None, 52, 52, 128) | 73,856 |
| max_pooling2d_8 (MaxPooling2D) | (None, 26, 26, 128) | 0 |
| flatten_2 (Flatten) | (None, 86528) | 0 |
| dense_4 (Dense) | (None, 128) | 11,075,712 |
| dropout_2 (Dropout) | (None, 128) | 0 |
| dense_5 (Dense) | (None, 1) | 129 |

**Total params:** 33,507,269 (127.82 MB)

**Trainable params:** 11,169,089 (42.61 MB)

**Non-trainable params:** 0 (0.00 B)

**Optimizer params:** 22,338,180 (85.21 MB)

**Fig. 3.** CNN Processing and its parameters

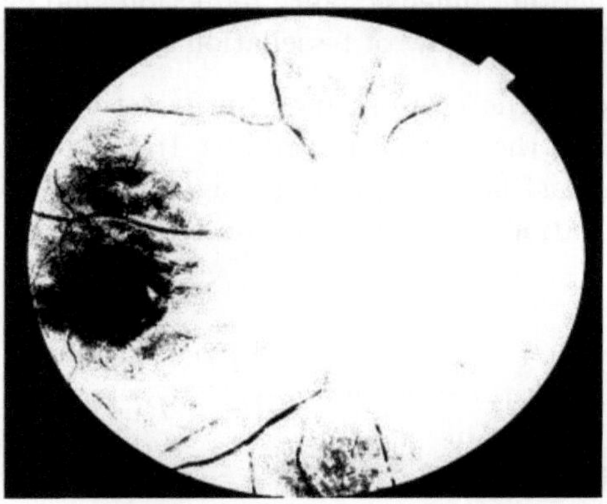

**Fig. 4.** Segmentation of Fundus Image

## 4 Experimental Analysis

**Data Preprocessing:** To make sure the input images are appropriate for CNN model training, the data preprocessing stage is essential. Our dataset consists of labeled images representing two classes: tessellated and non-tessellated patterns. Initially, we resize all images to a uniform dimension of 224x224 pixels to meet the input requirements of our CNN model.

**Normalization:** To make training more efficient, pixel values are scaled to a range of 0 to 1, which helps the model learn faster. Techniques like rotating, zooming, and flipping images vertically and horizontally are applied to further enhance the dataset.These techniques not only artificially increase the dataset size but also enhance the model's capacity to manage input image changes.

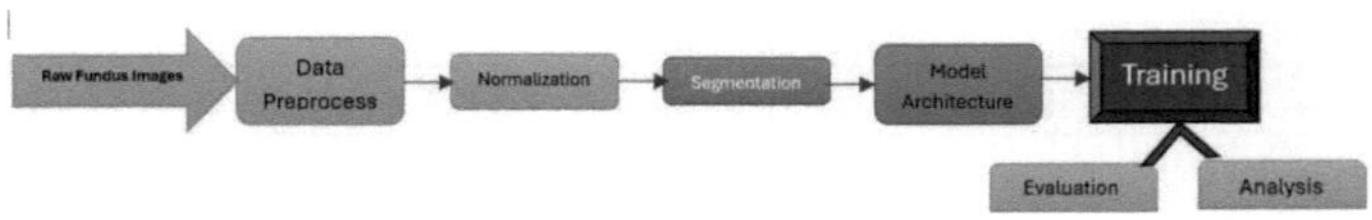


**Fig. 5.** Schematic workflow of Tessellation disease Detection

For tessellation identification, we employ a CNN model [13] that consists of three max-pooling layers and five convolutional layers. Each convolutional layer uses 3x3 filters with ReLU activation functions to extract features from the 224x224x3 pictures that are sent into the input layer. Max-pooling layers with a 2x2 pool size are used to minimize the feature maps, while dropout layers (rates of 0.25 and 0.5) are used to avoid overfitting. Two fully connected layers with 128 and 64 neurons combine features, and a final sigmoid activation function generates binary classification probabilities. This design maintains a balance between feature extraction, dimensionality reduction, and classification. [Fig. 5.] depicts about schematic workflow of tessellation disease detection

**Activation Function:** The network uses ReLU activation functions and max pooling layers to reduce the spatial dimensions. It also includes fully connected dense layers, with the last layer employing a sigmoid activation function to produce a binary classification: tessellated or non-tessellated.

**Precision**

$$\text{Precision} = \frac{TP}{TP + FP} \tag{1}$$

**Recall and Sensitivity**

$$\text{Recall \& Sensitivity} = \frac{TP}{TP + FN} \tag{2}$$

**Dataset.** Tessellated Fundus Disease Detection Using ConvNet" is a dataset of high-resolution fundus images that include the tessellated, which are often linked to a number of eye disorders. A retinal mosaic in aellated fundus may indicate a variety of retinal conditions. These photos have undergone processed to reduce noise and guarantee uniform lighting, matching the quality encountered in clinical settings.

The ground has been designated by skilled ophthalmologists to distinguish between sick and healthy fundus patterns due to the small alterations that may arise. With each image classified as either normal fundus or suggestive of

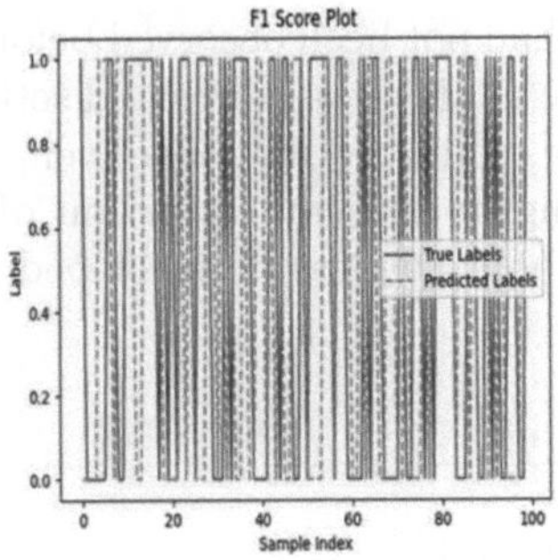


**Fig. 6.** Classification of F1 scores and recall

Tessellated Fundus Disease [Fig. 6.], this collection includes 12,500 photos from 200 individuals.

$$\text{Accuracy} = \frac{\text{Number of Correct Predictions}}{\text{Total Number of Predictions}} \tag{3}$$

# 5 Empirical Results and Discussions

The Convolutional Neural Network (CNN) model demonstrated exceptional performance in classifying tessellated images [Fig. 7.] when trained using a range of assessment metrics. The test accuracy of 91.7 successful in accurately differentiating between tessellated and non-tessellated patterns. Convergence is evident in the accuracy and loss curves for both the training and validation sets, indicating that the model was able to acquire the required features without experiencing appreciable overfitting.The picture [Fig. 8.] displaying model loss versus epochs illustrates the generalization and learning dynamics of the model. This example demonstrates how well the chosen neural network design and training parameters reduce the loss function across a number of epochs

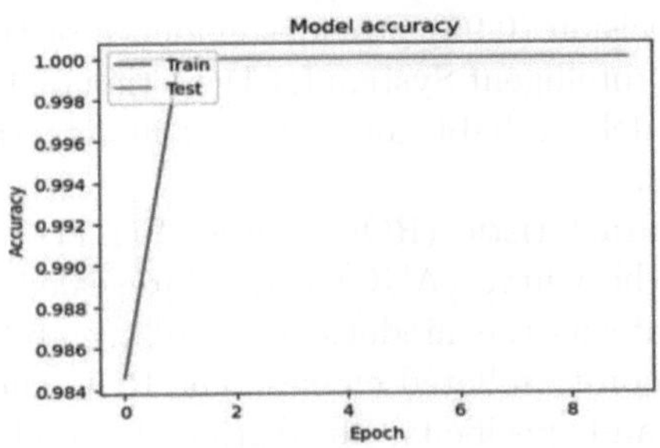


**Fig. 7.** Accuracy of Tessallation Classification.

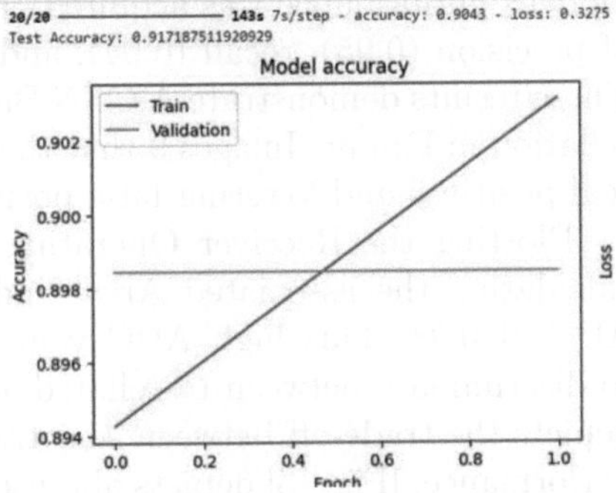


**Fig. 8.** Accuracy of Developed Model.

This study shows how the model gradually increased in forecast accuracy and durability over many epochs to reach a well-optimized state that permits good generalization to data that had not been observed before. Tessellated patterns are successfully classified by the model at all threshold settings.These comprehensive results provide strong proof of the model's effectiveness and imply that it might be used to issues pertaining to the categorization of pictures with tessellated patterns. [Fig. 9.] depicts about the loss of developed model.

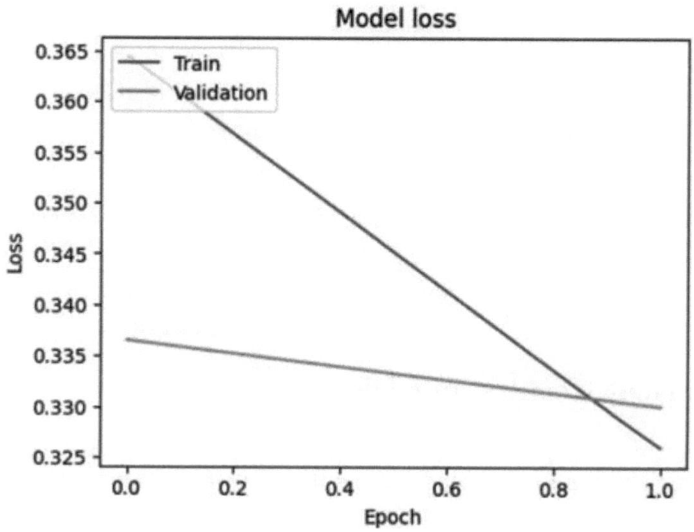


**Fig. 9.** Loss of developed Model

The confusion matrix [Fig. 10.], which shows high true positive and true negative rates, further supports the robustness of the concept. By computing the precision, recall, and F1 scores for every class, a thorough understanding of the model's performance was acquired. The model's balanced performance in terms of precision (0.95), recall (0.94), and precision (0.95) provides evidence of this. These results demonstrate A CNN Based Intelligent System for Detection of Tessellation in Fundus Images 9 that the model is reliable and accurate in detecting real positives and lowering false positives.

Plotting the Receiver Operating Characteristic (ROC) curve [Fig. 11] and calculating the associated Area Under the Curve (AUC) [Fig. 12.]revealed an AUC of 0.98. This high AUC value confirms the model's outstanding ability to discriminate between tessellated and non-tessellated classes. The ROC curve depicts the trade-off between sensitivity and specificity, illustrating the model's performance. [Fig. 13] depicts about classification report on the proposed model.

### 5.1 Challenges and Scope

**Data Heterogeneity:** Fundus images can differ based on patient characteristics, the imaging devices used, and the conditions present during data acquisi-

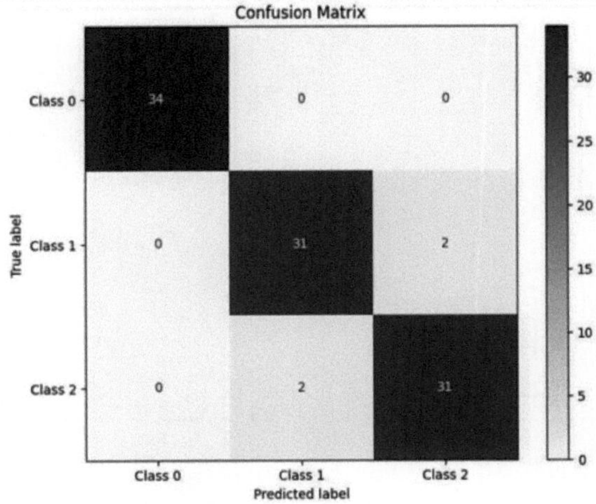


**Fig. 10.** Confusion Matrix

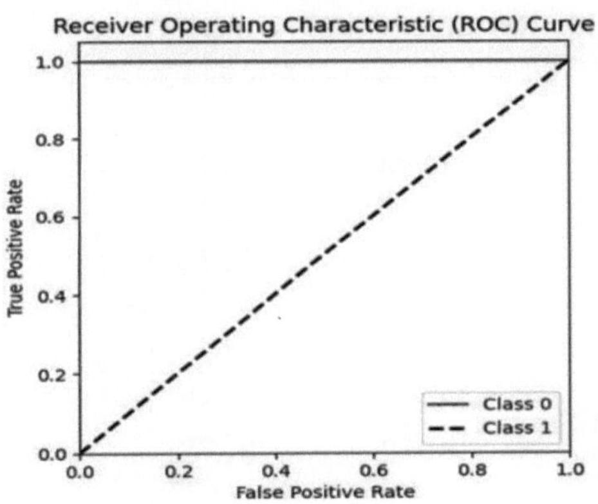


**Fig. 11.** ROC Curve

tion. This variability poses significant challenges in identifying fundus tessellation. To effectively normalize the data and enhance model performance, robust preprocessing and normalization techniques are crucial due to this unpredictability, which may result in varying detection and classification outcomes

**Feature Selection:** Relevant information from fundus photos is hard to extract in order to accurately depict tessellation patterns. More sophisticated feature selection methods are required to enhance the model's ability to distinguish between pathological and normal circumstances, reduce noise, and get rid of redundancy. This is even more important because image data is large dimensional.

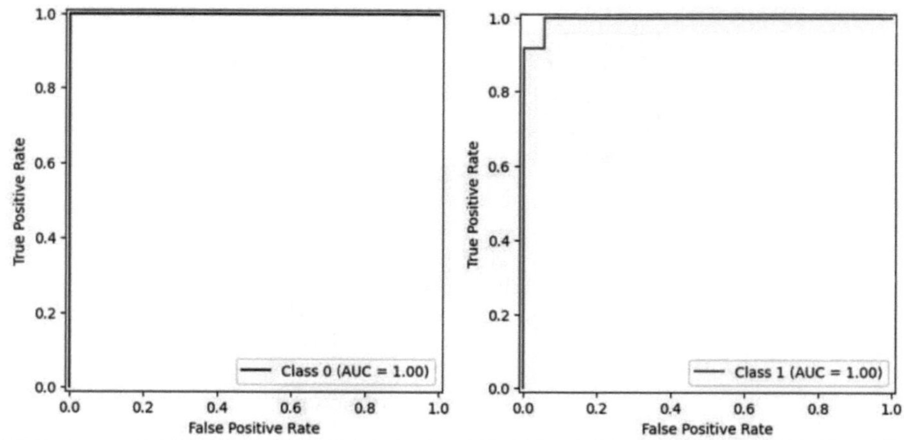


**Fig. 12.** AUC Rate Curve

```
F1 Score: 0.68
Classification Report:
              precision    recall  f1-score   support

     Class 0       1.00      1.00      1.00        11
     Class 1       0.63      1.00      0.77        12
     Class 2       0.00      0.00      0.00         7

    accuracy                           0.77        30
   macro avg       0.54      0.67      0.59        30
weighted avg       0.62      0.77      0.68        30
```

**Fig. 13.** Classification Report on the Proposed Model

**Unbalanced Data:** When developing and using machine learning models for fundus tessellation detection, it's important to handle patient data responsibly. Strong privacy protections must be in place, and all actions should comply with legal and ethical standards like GDPR and HIPAA. Following these rules is essential to safeguard patient information and stay legally compliant.n necessary to balance the data.

Forecasts that Do Not Fairly Consider Underrepresented Groups Uneven distributions of tessellated and non-tessellated data in datasets can cause bias in evaluation and training methods. Common solutions to this problem include class weight-changing algorithms, undersampling, and oversampling, which result in a more fair dataset with trustworthy results.

**Clinical Impact:** In order for model predictions to truly help in clinical settings, they must be verified against actual clinical results and incorporated into current diagnostic systems. It is essential to bridge the gap between theoretical understanding and real-world implementation in order to successfully integrate computational insights into healthcare.

## 6 Conclusion

Deep Convolutional Neural Networks (DCNNs) have transformed the study of fundus tessellations and other unique retinal patterns in ophthalmology.Doctors can more quickly and accurately identify connected eye diseases thanks to these networks' amazing capacity to pick up on subtle characteristics and trends.In addition to expediting the testing process, this technology helps doctors assess the severity and course of specific eye disorders. As a result, patients receive more individualized medications, fewer incorrect diagnoses, and improved treatment outcomes. DCNNs are also very good at identifying eye disorders associated with fundus tessellation since they are trained on a wide range of datasets.

## References

1. Li, R., et al.: Application of artificial intelligence to quantitative assessment of fundus tessellated density in young adults with different refractions. Ophthalmic Res. **66**(1), 710–720 (2023)
2. Huang, D., et al.: Prevalence of fundus tessellation and its screening based on artificial intelligence in Chinese children: the Nanjing eye study. Ophthalmol Therapy **12**(5), 2671–2685 (2023)
3. Shao, L., et al.: Prediction of the fundus tessellation severity with machine learning methods. Front. Med. **9**, 817114 (2022)
4. Wang, R., et al.: Efficacy of a deep learning system for screening myopic maculopathy based on color fundus photographs. Ophthalmol Therapy **12**(1), 469–484 (2023)
5. Lyu, X., Li, H., Zhen, Y., Ji, X., Zhang, S.: Deep tessellated retinal image detection using convolutional neural networks. In: 2017 39th Annual International Conference of the IEEE Engineering in Medicine and Biology Society (EMBC), pp. 676–680 (2017)
6. He, H.L., et al.: Fundus tessellated density of pathologic Myopia. Asia-Pacific J. Ophthalmol., 101097 (2022)
7. Wang, C., Zhang, M., Yang, L., et al.: Application of convolutional neural networks in fundus tessellation recognition. IEEE Access **9**, 53699–53708 (2021)
8. Wu, Q., Wang, Y., Zhang, X., et al.: Deep learning-based quantitative analysis of fundus tessellated density. IEEE Access **10**, 135312–135320 (2022)
9. Shao, L., et al.: Prediction of the fundus tessellation severity with machine learning methods. Front. Med. **9**, 817114 (2022)
10. Wang, R., et al.: Efficacy of a deep learning system for screening myopic maculopathy based on color fundus photographs. Ophthalmol. Therapy **12**(1), 469–484 (2023)

11. Liu, R., Yang, H.: Spatial tessellation of infectious disease spread for epidemic decision support. IEEE Robot. Autom. Lett. **7**(1), 626–633 (2021)
12. Zhang, Y., Wang, S., Liu, Q., et al.: Automated detection of fundus tessellation using deep learning techniques. IEEE Access **8**, 145632–145641 (2020)
13. Liu, J., Wu, X., Zhao, H., et al.: A novel machine learning approach for quantitative analysis of fundus tessellation. IEEE Access **9**, 29577–29586 (2021)
14. Sahu, B., Panigrahi, A., Rout, S.K.: DCNN-SVM: a new approach for lung cancer detection. In: Recent Advances in Computer Based Systems, Processes and Applications, pp. 97–105. CRC Press (2020)

# Alzheimer Disease Prediction: A Fusion of Clinical Health Records and Medical Imaging

Kwabena Ansah[1], Ampofo Twumasi[1], Joseph Agyapong Mensah[2], and Justice Kwame Appati[1](✉)

[1] Department of Computer Science, University of Ghana, Accra, Ghana
{kansah,atwumasi}@st.ug.edu.gh, jkappati@ug.edu.gh
[2] Department of Computer Science and Information Systems, Ashesi University, Berekuso, Ghana
jamensah@ashesi.edu.gh

**Abstract.** Research indicates that mild cognitive impairment (MCI) progresses to Alzheimer's disease at an estimated rate of 10–15% per year. A common symptom associated with this progression is memory loss. Traditionally, studies in this field have relied on a single type of data to predict the disease's occurrence. However, recent studies have shown pro4mising results when multiple data modalities are considered. Methodologically, standard convolutional neural networks (CNNs) are typically used in successful deep learning techniques. However, they often face challenges such as large parameter sizes, resulting in computationally expensive operations. In this study, we enhance the prediction performance of Alzheimer's disease by augmenting patient electronic health records (EHR) with magnetic resonance images (MRI), focusing on metrics like accuracy, precision, and recall. To achieve this, we utilized a stacked denoising autoencoder to generate intermediate relevant features from the patient's EHR. Concurrently, a depthwise separable convolutional network was employed to extract features from the patient's MRI data. Experimentally, this multimodal approach demonstrated significant improvements, recording an accuracy of 95.74%, a recall of 95.21%, and a precision of 95.00%, compared to classical CNNs used in existing networks.

**Keywords:** Alzheimer's Disease · Convolutional Neural Network · Magnetic Resonance Imaging · Depthwise Separable Convolutional Network · Electronic Health Record · Mild Cognitive Impairment

## 1 Introduction

Alzheimer's disease (AD) is a progressive neurodegenerative disorder that primarily affects older adults [9], and its prevalence is expected to increase significantly with the aging global population [15]. Mild cognitive impairment (MCI), a transitional phase preceding AD, converts to AD at an estimated annual rate of 10–15%. Despite extensive research, the underlying causes of AD remain elusive, and no current treatments can effectively halt or reverse its progression [17]. Therefore, emphasis has shifted toward


R. Kumar et al. (Eds.): ICNGCCA 2025, LNICST 665, pp. 75–88, 2026.
https://doi.org/10.1007/978-3-032-13009-9_7

early and accurate detection, particularly during predementia stages like MCI [18, 19]. Notably, some individuals with pathological signs of AD exhibit no cognitive impairment in later life [6], suggesting that the disease's pathogenic mechanisms may begin well before symptoms appear. Imaging biomarkers, especially those derived from MRI, play a vital role in early diagnosis. MRI offers detailed insights useful for detecting neurological disorders such as depression and schizophrenia [20]. The emergence of deep learning (DL), beginning with the introduction of the auto-encoder in 2006 [5], has transformed domains like computer vision, speech processing, and medical image analysis [2]. DL models have shown strong potential in clinical decision support for conditions such as cancer [7], diabetic retinopathy [4], and AD, by learning complex features directly from raw imaging data. CNN-based architectures, in particular, have been shown to outperform clinicians in AD prediction tasks [3, 14].

Although numerous studies focus on classifying subjects into AD, MCI, or normal controls (NC), fewer address the challenge of reducing DL model complexity [13]. Conventional CNNs, such as AlexNet with its 60 million parameters and 500,000 neurons [1], are computationally intensive and impractical for resource-constrained environments. To tackle this, [13] proposed a depthwise separable CNN (DSCNN) architecture that decomposes standard convolutions into more efficient operations, thereby reducing redundancy and computational load. While this approach lowered parameter counts, it incurred slight trade-offs in accuracy and recall. Moreover, most existing AD research relies on single-modality inputs—primarily MRI—which are costly and time-consuming to acquire [23]. CNNs also struggle when trained on limited datasets. To overcome these limitations, recent work advocates for multimodal approaches that combine neuroimaging with complementary data sources such as PET scans, cognitive assessments, demographic profiles, and clinical symptoms. Such integration has the potential to enhance prediction accuracy by mitigating data noise and uncertainty.

Motivated by these findings, the present study proposes a novel deep learning framework based on Depthwise Separable CNNs, designed to integrate MRI data with patient clinical records. This multimodal strategy aims to reduce model complexity while enhancing predictive performance for AD diagnosis. The rest of the study is sectioned as follows: Sect. 2 considered the reviews of some related studies while Sect. 3 presents the technical methodology adapted for the study. In Sect. 4 a detail experimental results was documented and finally we have Sect. 5 which concludes the study.

## 2 Related Works

This section reviews significant studies that utilize deep learning (DL) and ML for the detection and diagnosis of AD, alongside key developments in medical image analysis. In [24], a CNN model was developed using MRI scans from the ADNI 3 dataset to classify AD, mild cognitive impairment (MCI), and normal cases. Their dataset included 2,480 AD, 1,512 MCI, and 2,633 normal images. The study highlighted the superior performance of DL methods over traditional shallow ML techniques for large-scale medical data. Their model outperformed others that used the Open Access Series of Imaging Studies (OASIS) in terms of classification accuracy. Similarly, [25] employed a CNN to extract features from MRI scans and used a MultiClass Classifier to detect early AD stages. This approach achieved a 96% accuracy rate by identifying structural changes in the brain. In another study, [26] applied DL on structural MRI data from the GARD dataset, using a combination of CNN and DNN models to extract volumetric features from both brain hemispheres. The system yielded classification accuracies of 94.82% (left hippocampus) and 94.02% (right hippocampus), with AUCs of 92.54% and 90.62%, respectively.

Further, [27] proposed a CNN model for AD diagnosis using raw volumetric MRI data from 302 AD patients and 555 controls (ADNI dataset). They compared models with and without attention mechanisms to a 3D ResNet, achieving 91% accuracy. The model utilized 3D Gradient Weighted Class Activation Mapping (Grad-CAM) to highlight AD-relevant brain regions. To address computational efficiency, [13] introduced a depth-wise separable CNN (DSCNN) for AD classification using the OASIS dataset. The lightweight model, optimized for mobile devices, achieved notable accuracy improvements by incorporating elements from GoogleNet and AlexNet—resulting in nearly a 20% performance gain. In [11], a fully connected CNN was developed with a connection-wise attention mechanism. The method used stretched 3D convolutions to learn spatial features from preprocessed MRI images. It achieved classification accuracies of 97.35% for AD vs. controls, 87.82% for MCI converters vs. controls, and 78.79% for MCI converters vs. non-converters.

Lastly, [22] proposed a multimodal DL approach to stage AD by integrating MRI, electronic health records, and genetic data. They employed a 3D CNN for image analysis and a stacked denoising autoencoder [12] for clinical and genomic features. The model, trained on the ADNI dataset, demonstrated the effectiveness of deep models over shallow ones and identified critical regions such as the hippocampus, amygdala, and those involved in Rey Auditory Verbal Learning as highly predictive for AD.

## 3 Research Methodology and Study Design

This section outlines the theoretical foundations of the methods employed in this study. It covers the fundamental concepts of conventional machine learning and deep learning as applied to medical image processing. Detailed descriptions of the preprocessing pipelines for both MRI images and clinical records are provided, along with the training and optimization processes for all models utilized in the study. The architecture of a standard CNN is compared and contrasted with that of a depth-wise separable CNN (DSCNN). Finally, the structure of the proposed deep learning architecture is presented [21].

### 3.1 Data Description and Preprocessing

This study leverages data from the ADNI, accessible via adni.loni.usc.edu under the leadership of Michael W. Weiner in 2003. The ADNI is a public-private initiative designed to exmaine whether serial MRI & PET scans, other biomarkers, and clinical or cognitive assessments can monitor the progression of MCI and early AD. The imaging dataset comprises MRI and PET scans from the ADNI1, ADNI GO, and ADNI2 phases. Specifically, this work utilizes 2,294 standardized 1.5T MRI scans from the ADNI1 phase, representing 639 participants—some with multiple scans due to follow-up visits.

Each scan consists of 256 axial slices, forming a 3D image. For multimodal analysis, these imaging data are integrated with electronic health records (EHR) drawn from the ADNIMERGE CSV file, which compiles longitudinal health metrics such as patient age, gender, education, MMSE, and ADAS scores. The ADNIMERGE dataset includes 15,338 records and 113 features spanning 2,309 participants. While every patient with MRI data has associated EHRs, the reverse does not always hold. The 'DX_bl' column identifies baseline clinical diagnoses, categorizing subjects as early MCI (EMCI), late MCI (LMCI), or SMC. For the purpose of binary classification focused on AD detection, LMCI, EMCI, and SMC cases are consolidated into a single MCI group. Only baseline visit entries were used, and patients with missing 'DX_bl' values were excluded. After filtering, 2,295 participants with complete clinical records were retained for preprocessing. Participant distribution was stratified according to diagnostic labels derived from the EHR data.

### 3.1.1 Research Tools

The MRI dataset undergoes pre-processing to ensure optimal prediction performance when fed into the CNN models. The tools utilized for MRI image pre-processing include the Deep Learning Toolkit (DLTK), SimpleITK, SimpleElastix, and the FMRIB Software Library Brain Extraction Tool (FSL BET).

### 3.1.2 Pre-processing Steps (MRI Data)

The following steps were carried out in this study in processing the MRI data. These steps are (Fig. 1): Spatial Normalization, Image registration, and Skull Stripping,

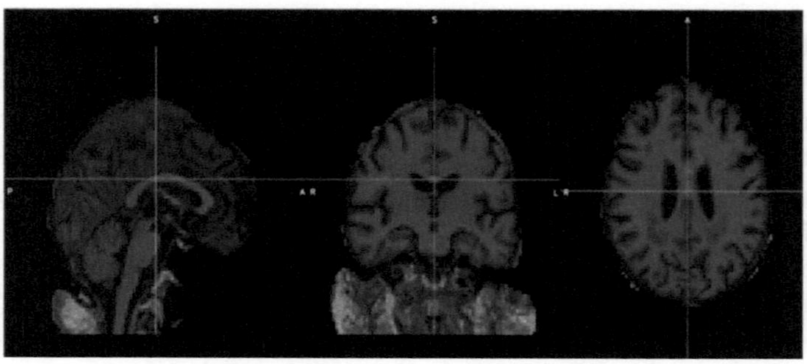

**Fig. 1.** Sagittal, coronal, axial cuts of a single MRI image after spatial normalization, registration, and skull stripping

### 3.1.3 Selection of Image Slice from 3D Image for 2D CNN Models

After pre-processing, the images were in 3D form, which made them only suitable for 3D CNN architectures. To convert them to 2D images that would be compatible with the 2D CNN models used in this work, the 45th slice of all the 3D images from the axial view was selected after careful analysis.

### 3.1.4 Clinical/Electronic Health Records

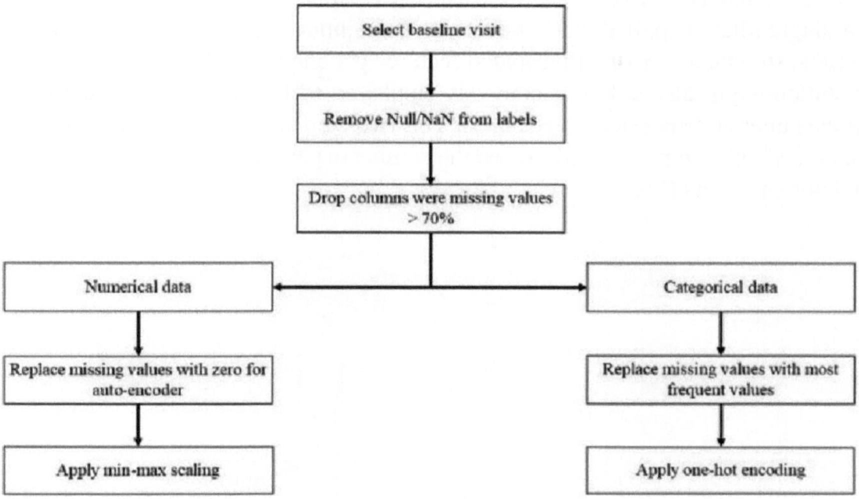


**Fig. 2.** Pre-processing pipeline for electronic health records

As stated earlier, only clinical records collected at baseline visits are used in this work. Also, labels for clinical records are stored in the "DX_bl" column of the ADNIMERGE.csv dataset. The pipeline for the processing of the data is shown in Fig. 2.

### 3.1.5 Label Encoding

As stated earlier, this study focuses on diagnosing the disease rather than studying its progression. For this study, we let CN, SMC, LMCI, AD, and EMCI represent Controls, Subjective memory compliant, Late mild cognitive impairment, Alzheimer's disease and Early mild cognitive impairment respectively. Table 1 describes the values assigned to each label as its codes.

**Table 1.** Label encoding for clinical records

| Label | CN (controls) | EMCI | LMCI | SMC |
|---|---|---|---|---|
| Encodings | 0 | 1 | 1 | 1 |

## 3.2 Depthwise Separable Convolutional Neural Networks (DSCNN) and Computations Involved

Depthwise Separable Convolutional Neural Networks (DSCNNs) offer an efficient alternative to the classical conv layers by breaking the convolution process into two distinct operations: pointwise convolution and depthwise convolution. Unlike conventional convolution, which simultaneously processes spatial and channel dimensions, DSCNNs aim to reduce redundancy by handling these aspects separately.

A single filter is applied independently to each input channel at the depthwise convolutional step thereby extracting spatial features per channel. After which a pointwise convolution—typically a 1 × 1 conv—is employed to linearly combine the outputs from the depthwise stage across channels. This two-step approach leads to a substantial reduction in both computational cost and the number of parameters compared to standard convolutional layers (Fig. 3).

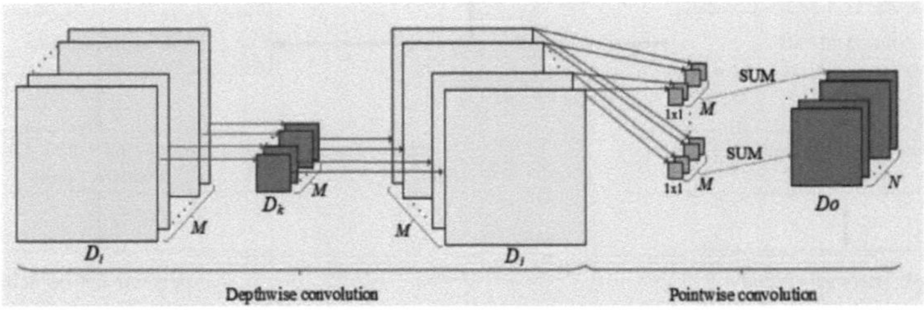


**Fig. 3.** Structure of DSCNN including depthwise and pointwise convolution modules [13]

For example, given a zero padding with a unit stride applied on a single filter, the depthwise convolution captures localized features, and the pointwise convolution aggregates these into a final representation. The output feature maps generated by this process can be mathematically represented in Eq. 1:

$$\phi_{k,l,m} = \sum_{i,j} K_{i,j,m}.I_{k+i-1,l+j-1,m} \tag{1}$$

where, $I$ refers to the input feature map, $\phi$ the resulting output, and $K$ the kernel for convolution. The indices $i$ and $j$ denote positions within the kernel, while $k$ and $l$ locate positions in the input and output maps. The index $m$ corresponds to the channel number. The number of parameters and cost function for depthwise convolution is represented as Eq. 2 and Eq. 3:

$$P_2 = M \times D_k^2 \tag{2}$$

$$C_2 = M \times D_i^2 \times D_k^2 \tag{3}$$

The number of parameters and cost for depthwise and pointwise convolution combined is represented mathematically by Eq. 4 and Eq. 5, respectively as:

$$P_3 = M \times D_k^2 + M \times N \tag{4}$$

$$C_3 = M \times D_i^2 \times D_k^2 + M \times N \times D_i^2 \tag{5}$$

The reduction in computational cost ($C_,$) and number of parameters ($P_,$) is expressed as Eq. 6 and 7:

$$P_4 = P_3 - P = M \times D_k^2 + M \times N - M \times N \times D_k^2 \tag{6}$$

$$C_4 = C_4 - C = M \times D_i^2 \times D_k^2 + M \times N \times D_i^2 - M \times N \times D_i^2 \times D_k^2 \tag{7}$$

### 3.3 Stacked Denoising Auto-Encoder (SDAE)

In this study, we employ the Stacked Denoising Autoencoder (SDAE), as illustrated in Fig. 9, to classify patients into three diagnostic categories: CN, MCI, and AD, using data derived from the EHR.

A standard Autoencoder (AE) is designed to learn a representation by reconstructing its input, but its sensitivity to noise can limit its performance. To overcome this limitation, Denoising Autoencoders (DAEs) were introduced [10], aiming to extract more robust features. A DAE is composed of 3 layers: the output, hidden and input layer. The model operates in two phases—encoding and decoding. During the encoding phase, the input $x$ is transformed into a hidden representation $y$ using a nonlinear activation function $s$, as defined in Eq. 8:

$$f_\theta(x) = s(Wx + b) \tag{8}$$

Here, $\theta = \{W, b\}$, where $W$ is the weight matrix and $b$ is the bias vector. Common choices for the activation function $s$ include sigmoid, tanh, and ReLU.

In the decoding phase, the hidden representation is mapped back to reconstruct the input, producing the output $z$. This process is given by Eq. 9:

$$g_{\theta'}(y) = s(W'y + b') \tag{9}$$

where $\theta' = \{W', b'\}$. The decoding parameters $W'$ and $b'$ may either be independent from or tied to the transpose of the encoding parameters.

Rather than aiming for perfect input reconstruction, DAEs attempt to learn a latent representation $z$ that captures the underlying structure of the data. From an information-theoretic standpoint, minimizing reconstruction error helps preserve essential aspects of the input, but naive reconstruction (e.g., simply learning $y = x$) fails to extract meaningful features. Introducing noise into the input and training the model to recover the original signal encourages the network to learn more informative representations.

The concept of stacking DAEs resembles the layer-wise pretraining strategy used in Deep Belief Networks (DBNs). The stacking procedure begins by training the first denoising autoencoder using the original input and its first hidden layer. The trained parameters are then used to initialize the corresponding layers in the deeper model. This process is repeated for subsequent hidden layers, each time using the output from the previous layer as input [8]. Once all layers are initialized, the model is fine-tuned using the clean, uncorrupted data for forward propagation and classification (Fig. 4).

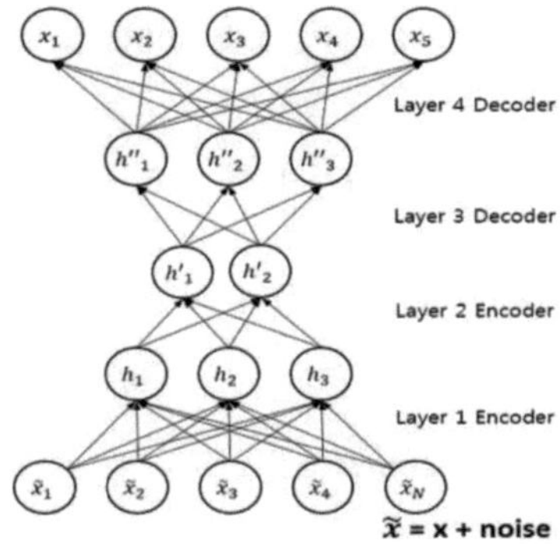


**Fig. 4.** Stacked denoising auto-encoder

# 4 Results and Discussion

In this section, the evaluation metrics used for the model performance assessment is outlined. It also details the partitioning of the MRI and image datasets into train, validate, and test subsets, as well as the fine-tuning strategies employed to enhance model accuracy. A performance comparison is made between the CNN and the DSCNN. Additionally, the effectiveness of the proposed multimodal approach is evaluated against single-modality methods, specifically the DSCNN and the Stacked Denoising Autoencoder (SDAE), used in this study.

## 4.1 Experimental Results for Standard CNN and DSCNN on MRI Data

The image dataset was divided into 15% for testing and 85% for both training and validation. Hyperparameters such as dropout rates, the sizes and number of convolutional kernels at each layer, and the sizes of pooling kernels for each layer were tuned. On the validation dataset, we fixed the values of the remaining hyperparameters and selected the value with the best accuracy for each one. This process was repeated several times until the performance stabilized. Both standard and depthwise separable CNNs were trained for three-class classification: CN, MCI, and AD, over 100 epochs. By the end of the 100th epoch, the training loss was 0.5930, and the validation loss was 0.7642. The training and validation accuracies were 0.7664 and 0.6776, respectively. In comparison, the DSCNN produced a training accuracy of 0.7524 and a validation accuracy of 0.6503, which were slightly lower than those achieved by the standard CNN. Figures 5 and 6 illustrate (a) the training and validation accuracy (on the x-axis) against several epochs (on the y-axis) and (b) the convergence of standard and DSCNN, respectively.

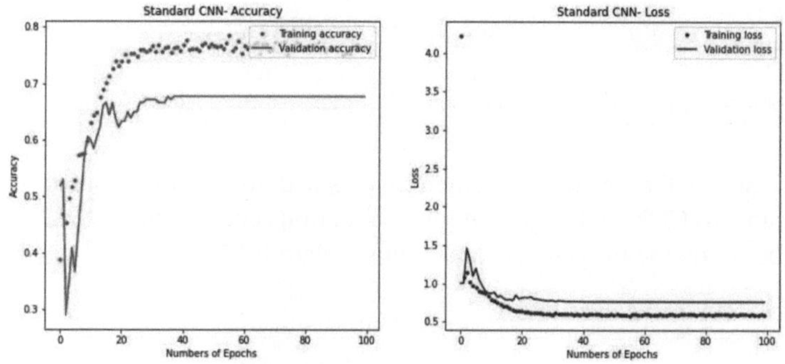


**Fig. 5.** Training history of standard CNN

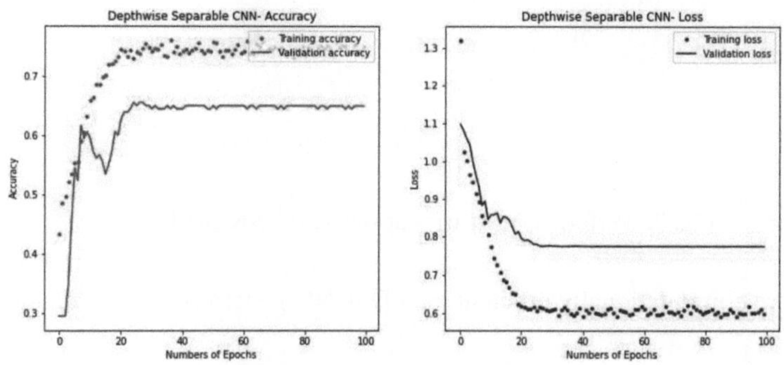


**Fig. 6.** Training history of DSCNN

Depthwise separable and standard CNN were fine-tuned to have the same hyper-parameter. This was to ensure that none of them was at a natural disadvantage. After fine-tuning, dropout was set as 0.25 for all the layers. Table 3 shows the combination of trials to achieve the final model for the standard CNN and DSCNN. The size of the kernel for max-pooling was $2 \times 2$ throughout training and fine-tuning (Table 2).

**Table 2.** Different hyperparameter values tried for both standard, and Depthwise separable CNN are shown in this table.

| Hyperparameters | Types | Values |
|---|---|---|
| Convolutional kernel sizes | Initial Training | $2 \times 2, 4 \times 4$ |
| | Fine Tuning | $3 \times 3$ |
| Dropout Value | All Layers | 0.6, 0.4, 0.3, 0.25 |
| Number of filters | Layer 1 | 128, 32 |
| | Layer 2 | 256, 64, 512, 128 |
| | Layer 3 | 512, 256 |

*(continued)*

**Table 2.** (*continued*)

| Hyperparameters | Types | Values |
|---|---|---|

Figure 7 shows the performance metrics of standard CNN compared to DSCNN. Although standard CNN had slightly higher validation accuracy than DSCNN, DSCNN performed better on the unseen test data than standard CNN.

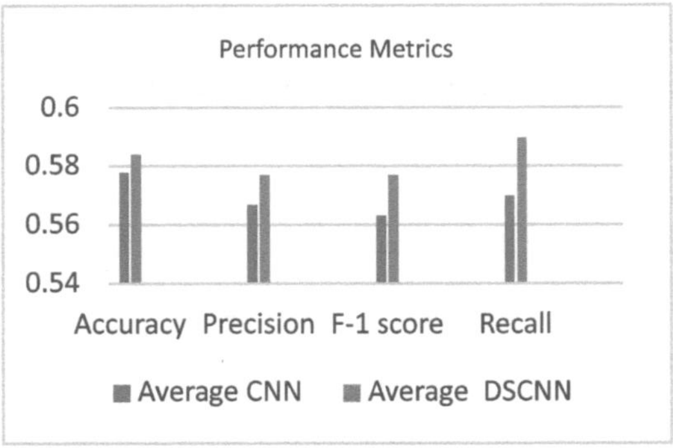


**Fig. 7.** Performance metrics of standard CNN and DSCNN

It is more computationally efficient than DSCNN generalizing well on the test data.

### 4.2 Computational Performance of CNN and DSCNN

The ratio of cost of computation of DSCNN to standard CNN can be expressed as Eq. 10:

$$\frac{D_k^2+N}{D_k^2\times N}=\frac{1}{N}+\frac{1}{D_k^2} \tag{10}$$

where N = depth of output feature volume, D = dimension of kernel.

In this study, the ratio is 0.1144. That means standard CNN uses almost 9 times more computing power than DSCNN. In other words, the number of multiplications in DSCNN is reduced by 88.56%

### 4.3 Experimental Results for Denoising Auto-Encoder on Clinical Records (SDAE)

In accordance with Sect. 3.1, there exist only 639 patients possessing both MRI and clinical data. The clinical records of these 639 patients serve as the dataset for training and testing the SDAE model. The clinical records undergo a split, allocating 85% for training and validation, and 15% for testing purposes. The complete SDAE model, encompassing both the decoder and encoder components, undergoes optimization using the Adam optimizer and employs mean squared error (MSE) as the loss function, utilizing the training set. Subsequently, the encoder segment of the fully trained SDAE is isolated and preserved. A softmax layer is introduced to this preserved encoder layer for the purpose of three-class classification. The pertinent parameters utilized in the SDAE setup are detailed in Table 3, while the outcomes are delineated in Table 4.

**Table 3.** Different hyperparameter values for SDAE

| Hyperparameters | Types | Values |
|---|---|---|
| Dropout Value | For each Layer | 0.8, 0.4, 0.3, 0.6 |
| Number of neurons | Layer 1 | 300, 250 |
| | Layer 2 | 250, 150 |
| | Layer 3 (bottleneck layer) | 100, 50 |

**Table 4.** Performance metrics of SDAE on clinical/electronic health records

| Metric | Accuracy | Recall | Precision | F1-score |
|---|---|---|---|---|
| SDAE | 0.9304 | 0.9300 | 0.9300 | 0.9301 |

### 4.4 Multimodal Analysis

As previously mentioned, the multimodal architecture integrates intermediate features from both DSCNN and SDAE. Within this architecture, it becomes evident that the intermediate features derived from DSCNN possess a dimensionality of 256. This dimensionality stems from utilizing the output of the last fully connected layer of DSCNN as an intermediate feature for images within the multimodal architecture. Following the removal of the softmax layer, the output of the encoder segment of SDAE functions as the intermediate feature for clinical records. This aims to ascertain whether SDAE identifies any latent relationships within intermediate clinical data that may not be readily apparent in the raw clinical data. To assess whether the intermediate features generated by SDAE effectively uncover hidden relationships within the data, a clustering-based approach is employed. Specifically, k-means clustering is applied to the intermediate features derived from electronic health records (EHR). This methodology aims to detect any subtle associations captured by the intermediate features that may not be evident in the raw data. The determination of the optimal cluster number is conducted using both the elbow method and silhouette coefficient method, as illustrated in Figs. 8 and 9.

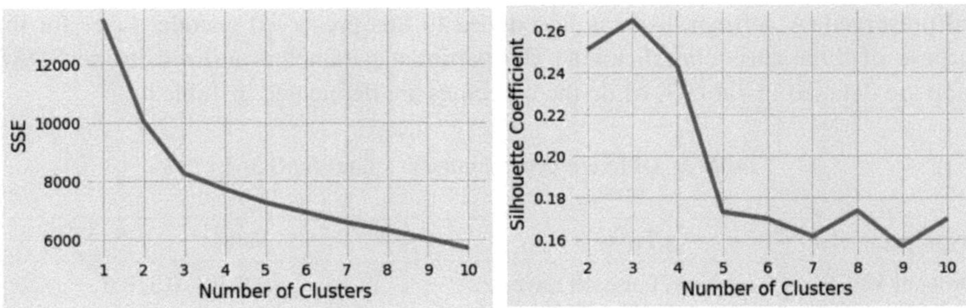


**Fig. 8.** Evaluation of cluster number using elbow method (left) and silhouette coefficient (right).

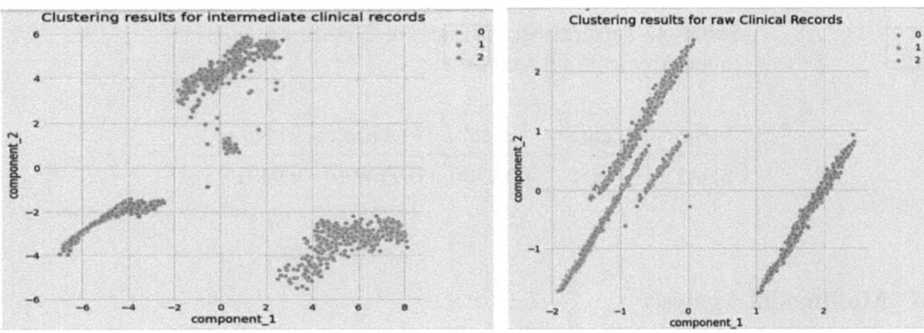


**Fig. 9.** Intermediate features of clinical records (left), raw clinical data (right)

### 4.5 Performance of Multimodal Architecture

**Table 5.** Performance of multimodal architecture

| Metric | Accuracy | Recall | Prediction | F1-score |
|---|---|---|---|---|
| Proposed Multimodal Architecture | 0.9574 | 0.9521 | 0.9500 | 0.9500 |

The experimental findings outlined in Table 5 highlight that the proposed multimodal architecture attains superior accuracy, precision, recall, and F1-score when compared to individual modality architectures—specifically, DSCNN and SDAE. This section has underscored that DSCNN exhibits greater computational efficiency and delivers competitive performance in contrast to the standard CNN. Furthermore, a clusteringbased analysis has been employed to showcase the stacked denoising autoencoder's capacity to discern relationships that remain concealed within raw clinical data. Lastly, it is observed that the utilization of random forest at the classification layer within the multimodal architecture yields enhanced performance compared to singlemodality approaches.

## 5 Conclusion

This study introduces a computationally efficient multimodal deep learning framework for Alzheimer's disease prediction, leveraging MRI and clinical patient data. Intermediate data for this framework is derived from MRI scans and clinical health records utilizing depthwise separable CNN and stacked denoising autoencoder models. A comparison between standard CNN and DSCNN reveals that DSCNN achieves competitive performance with reduced computational requirements, making it an ideal choice for extracting intermediate features from pre-processed MRI images in the ADNI dataset. Following a 3-class classification (CN for normal, MCI for mild cognitive impairment, and AD for Alzheimer's disease), experimental findings showcase the superiority of the proposed deep multimodal architecture over the deep single modality architectures employed in this study.

## References

1. Alex, K., Ilya, S., Geoffrey, E.H.: ImageNet classification with deep convolutional neural networks. Adv. Neural Inf. Process. Syst. **25**, 1097–1105 (2016)
2. Bengio, Y., Courville, A., Vincent, P.: Representation learning: a review and new perspectives. IEEE Trans. Pattern Anal. Mach. Intell. **35**(8), 1798–1828 (2013)
3. Bijen, K., Goo-Rak, K.: 3D CNN design for the classification of alzheimer's disease using brain MRI and PET. IEEE Access **8**, 217830–217847 (2020)
4. Esteva, A., Kuprel, B., Novoa, R.A., Justin Ko, S.M., Blau, H.M., Thrun, S.: Dermatologist-level classification of skin cancer with deep neural networks. Nature **542**, 115–118 (2017)
5. Geoffrey, E.H., Simon, O., Teh, Y.-W.: A fast learning algorithm for deep belief nets. Neural Comput. **18**, 1527–1554 (2006)
6. Goldman, W.P., et al.: Absence of cognitive impairment or decline in preclinical Alzheimer's disease. Neurology **56**(3), 361–367 (2001)
7. Gulshan, V., Peng, L., Coram, M., Derek, W., Arunachalam, N., Stumpe, M.C.: Development and validation of a deep learning algorithm for detection of diabetic retinopathy in retinal fundus photographs. JAMA **316**, 2402–2410 (2016)
8. Hao-ran, Q., Ji-imng, L., Jun-yi, W.: Stacked denoising autoencoders applied to star/galaxy classification. Chin. Astron. Astrophys. **41**, 282–292 (2017)
9. Hardey, J.: Alzheimer's disease: the amyloid cascade hypothesis—an update and reappraisal. J. Alzheimer's Dis. **9**, 151–153 (2006)
10. Hinton, G.E., Salakhutdinov, R.R.: Reducing the dimensionality of data with neural networks. Science **313**, 504–507 (2006)
11. Jie, Z., Bowen, Z., Ang, G., Xin, F., Dong, L., Xiaojing, L.: A 3D densely connected convolution neural network with connection-wise attention mechanism for Alzheimer's disease classification. Magn. Reson. Imaging **78**, 119–126 (2021)
12. Jun, S., Zheng, X., Yan, L., Zhang, Q., Ying, S.: Multimodal neuroimaging feature learning with multimodal stacked deep polynomial networks for diagnosis of alzheimer's disease. IEEE Access **22**, 173–183 (2018). https://doi.org/10.1109/JBHI.2017.2655720
13. Liu, J., Li, M., Luo, Y., Yang, S., Li, W., Bi, Y.: Alzheimer's disease detection using depthwise separable convolutional neural networks. Comput. Methods Prog. Biomed. **203**, 106032 (2021)
14. Klöppel, S., et al.: Accuracy of dementia diagnosis—a direct comparison between radiologists and a computerized method. Brain **131**, 2969–2974 (2008)

15. Kruthika, K.R., Maheshappa, H.D.: CBIR system using Capsule Networks and 3D CNN for Alzheimer's disease diagnosis. Inf. Med. Unlocked **14**, 59–68 (2019)
16. Michael, D.G., Gaurav, S.A., Menon, V.: Default-mode network activity distinguishes Alzheimer's disease from healthy aging: evidence from functional MRI. Proc. Natl. Acad. Sci. USA **101**, 4637–4642 (2004)
17. Morle, J., SA, F., Nguyen, A.: Alzheimer disease . Clin. Geriat. Med. 129–135 (2018)
18. Plant, C., et al.: Automated detection of brain atrophy patterns based on MRI for the prediction of Alzheimer's disease. NeuroImage **50**, 16–174 (2010)
19. Ju, R., Hu, C., Li, Q.: Early diagnosis of alzheimer's disease based on resting-state brain networks and deep learning. IEEE/ACM Trans. Comput. Biol. Bioinf. **16**(1), 244–257 (2017)
20. Rosa, M.J., et al.: Sparse network-based models for patient classification using fMRI. Neuroimage **105**, 493–506 (2015)
21. Roshanzamir, A., Aghajan, H., Soleymani Baghshah, M.: Transformer-based deep neural network language models for Alzheimer's disease risk assessment from targeted speech. BMC Med. Inf. Decis. Mak. **21**(1), 92 (2021)
22. Venugopalan, J., Tong, L., Hassanzadeh, H.R., Wang, M.D.: Multimodal deep learning models for early detection of Alzheimer's disease stage. Sci. Rep. **11**(1), 3254 (2021)
23. Yong, F., Nematollah, B., Chris, M.C., Christos, D.: Spatial patterns of brain atrophy in MCI patients, identified via high-dimensional pattern classification, predict subsequent cognitive decline. NeuroImage **39**, 1731–1743 (2008)
24. Salehi, A.W., Baglat, P., Sharma, B.B., Upadhya, A., Gupta, G.: A CNN model : earlier diagnosis and classification of alzheimer disease using MRI. In: Icosec, pp. 156–161 (2020)
25. Surendran, D., Karthiga, V., Monica, K.B., Pooja, R.: Alzheimer's disease diagnosis based on ensemble of multi-model convolutional neural networks. In 2021 5th International Conference on Trends in Electronics and Informatics (ICOEI), pp. 1451–1457 (2021)
26. Basher, A., Kim, B.C., Lee, K.H., Jung, H.Y.: Volumetric feature-based alzheimer's disease diagnosis from sMRI data using a convolutional neural network and a deep neural network. IEEE Access **9**, 29870–29882 (2021)
27. Ullanat, V., Balamurali, V., Rao, A.: A novel residual 3-D convolutional network for alzheimer's disease diagnosis based on raw MRI scans. In: 2020 IEEE-EMBS Conference on Biomedical Engineering and Sciences (IECBES), pp. 82–87 (2021)

# Impact of Aviation Advancements on Economics and Environment

Lakshya Bishnoi(✉)

Jumeirah College, Dubai, United Arab Emirates
lakshya.mr.b@gmail.com

**Abstract.** While the aviation industry has made notable advancements in areas such as aircraft design, engine efficiency, and sustainable aviation fuels, it still faces challenges in keeping up with the rapidly growing demand for air travel and the evolving needs of passengers. The pace of innovation may not always match the speed of demand, leaving room for further improvements to meet the increasing needs and challenges of the industry. As a result, this research paper explores the impact of the advancements in the aviation industry, with a specific focus on electric aviation, and aims to fill this gap in knowledge. Through an examination of safety regulations, aircraft capabilities, economic considerations, and technological advancements, this study seeks to understand the implications of electric aviation within the broader context of the aviation sector. The discussion encompasses various forms of aviation, including gas-powered aircraft, and highlights the nuanced interplay of economic, technological, and environmental factors. The analysis acknowledges the complexity of the industry and the multitude of variables involved, recognizing that advancements in electric aviation cannot be viewed in isolation. Rather, they must be evaluated in terms of their potential to drive economic growth, foster sustainability, and revolutionise air travel. By harnessing the power of electric propulsion systems, aircraft manufacturers aim to reduce greenhouse gas emissions and decrease reliance on fossil fuels, aligning with global sustainability goals. This study contributes to the ongoing discourse on the role of electric aviation in shaping the future of the aviation industry.

**Keywords:** Electric aircraft · aviation · Aviation economics · Aviation functionality · Sustainable aviation technology · SDG

## 1 Introduction

Electric aviation, characterised by the utilisation of electric propulsion systems to power aircraft, represents a frontier of innovation within the aviation sector. This research paper embarks on a comprehensive exploration of electric aviation, delving into its technological intricacies, economic implications, and environmental imperatives. This dissertation examines how developments in gas-powered aircraft and other emerging forms of aviation serve as reference points for evaluating the progress of electric flight technology. Key areas of focus include safety regulations, aircraft capabilities, and environmental considerations, with a particular emphasis on dissecting the components of electric aircraft,


R. Kumar et al. (Eds.): ICNGCCA 2025, LNICST 665, pp. 89–100, 2026.
https://doi.org/10.1007/978-3-032-13009-9_8

such as batteries and flight technology. In tandem with technological considerations, this project delves into the economic dimensions of electric aviation and investigates the pace of integration of electric aircraft into existing fleets and analyses the resultant impacts on primary economic agents. Electric aviation emerges as a promising solution to reduce greenhouse gas emissions and lessen reliance on fossil fuels. This paradigm shift not only aligns with global sustainability objectives but also offers opportunities for technological innovation and economic growth. As governments, businesses, and consumers prioritise sustainability, the demand for electric aircraft is anticipated to surge, thereby propelling further advancements in the industry. The objectives of this research paper are, to summarize the available literature on impact of advancements in electric aircraft and to identify the impact of advancements on functionality and economics of airline industry. As a methodology this paper is basic research based on secondary data and is descriptive by research design. Authenticated research data resources such a Scopus, google scholar, IEEE explore were used to identify and filter the suitable articles.

## 2 Literature Review

The review of literature summarizes the available knowledge in the aviation industry. Systematic literature review method was used to obtain the summary of published information in the following headings.

### 2.1 Engine Types that Utilize Gas-Powered Aircraft

Jack L. Kerrebrock (1996) published "Aircraft Engines and Gas Turbines" providing a straightforward explanation of the fundamental characteristics of gas turbines and their relevance to propulsion systems for aeroplanes [1]. Furthermore, the three most common engine classifications are appointed under the broad bracket of Heat Engines, as they all utilise thermal energy from the combustion of air. The three main engine types: turbojets, turboprops, and turbofans are selected based on configurations that balance other factors, particularly during different flying situations, and overall efficiency. Sanjay Garg in his research provides an overview of the aircraft turbine engine control research at NASA Glenn Research Center [2]. Much of the technology mentioned in the paper has been built by the founding principles highlighted in Kerrebrock's book and has been developed for increased safety and efficiency.

### 2.2 Functioning of Turbojet Engine

A research by Simon Fahlström and Rikard Pihl-Roos (2016) [3] deals with researching, A research project written by Simon Fahlström and Rikard Pihl-Roos, titled 'Design and Construction of a Simple Turbojet Engine" [3] deals with researching, designing and building jet engines [4]. The project delineates the fundamental processes that are common to all three types of jet engines: Turbojet, Turboprop, and Turbofan. The turbojet differs slightly from the other two engines in that its turbine is directly linked to a compressor. This distinction is particularly noticeable as it entails a somewhat more rudimentary design compared to both the turboprop and turbofan engines. However, the science of jet engines is still to a large degree an empirical one, where experimental data and a good amount of trial and error are needed to push the field forward.

### 2.3 Functioning of Turboprop Engine

Turboprop engines are unique due to their very high propulsive efficiency, however, this engine is mainly utilised in low-speed flight vehicles. If a turboprop is used to drive a propeller, it is mainly used for small aircraft and specialised logistics. Due to this engine's particular characteristics, it is used to keep costs down, specifically when utilised in the automotive industry. The reason for the high propulsive efficiency of the turboprop engine is due to the exhaust gas being cooled down to match the temperature of the air coming out of the compressor. This cooling process is unique and helps increase engine efficiency. This is one of the few differentiators between the other engines.

### 2.4 Functioning of Turbofan Engine

The first step for the turbofan engine to operate is the fan rotor pulling in air. In aeroplanes with former engines such as the turbojet engine, all the air would have been pulled into a series of parts to make the engine work. With a turbofan engine, the air is separated into two parts. One portion of the air is directed through the engine to drive its operation, while the other portion circumvents the engine and is expelled through a nozzle mechanism. The air that isn't pulled into the engine but surrounds it is called the "sheat flow" and is a cool layer of air that is responsible for 80 per cent of the aeroplane's thrust. This process decreases a high percentage of the noise that the engine makes and also provides high efficiency. The second step required for the turbofan engine to operate is the "compression" of the air that flows into the engine. The second step (compression) requires two parts, the low-pressure compressor and the high-pressure compressor. The low-pressure compressor begins the process of compacting the air just enough for the high-pressure compressor to complete the process effectively. The high-pressure compressor achieves this task with remarkable efficiency while maintaining a lightweight construction, attributed to its innovative design where the blades and disk are integrated into a single piece. The third step of the operation is the combustion, Once the air is compressed, it goes into a part of the engine called the combustor. In the combustor, there are nozzles that spray fuel into the compressed air, and this mixture of fuel and air catches fire. The temperature rises to about 1,700 degrees Celsius. This intense heat makes the gas expand and rush out of the combustor at a high velocity. The final step – expulsion – occurs when the hot gas rushes through two sets of turbines: high-pressure and low-pressure turbines. As the blades spin, the engine uses some energy to drive the booster, compressor and fan. After this, the hot gas exits through the thrust nozzle, giving an extra push to make the airplane propel forward.

### 2.5 Economic Benefits of Electric Aircraft

Michael J Cronin in the research discusses the advancements required to transition from gas-powered engines to electric engines as well as their benefits [5]. Cronin highlights that the prospect of electric aircraft supplies very attractive fuel-savings and aircraft support/acquisition cost reductions. He further implores that all-electric airplanes are well justified and a well-directed utilisation of national income. This is further supported by a contractor report referenced in the article, published by NASA [6]. Research states that not only was weight reduced, but there were other significant benefits to the total airplane design: maintenance costs, first costs, and airplane design costs were all reduced by the introduction of this technology (referring to the technology utilised to create an all-electric aircraft). Furthermore, the study mentions that out of all the seven technologies studied, the all-electric airplane was the one which was found to have a clear-cut payoff. This implies that through the decades of research and development performed by NASA, the all-electric aircraft is the most viable due to its economic benefits.

### 2.6 Propulsion Systems and Economic Viability

G. Philip Salle [7] in his research presents the results of a detailed analysis of current propulsion system maintenance costs directed at determining the trends in costs with advances in engine technology. The report meticulously analyses the fuel costs, to simplify this section of the report to a limited extent, high-performance engines lose efficiency faster than lower-performance ones. Maintenance costs are based on this loss. In light of escalating fuel costs, the prospect of investing more in maintenance to enhance fuel efficiency emerges as a viable consideration, albeit hindered by the absence of such technology at present. One of the methods of depicting the reliability of the source is the publisher of the report, the National Aeronautics and Space Administration NASA NTRS - NASA Technical Reports Server [8].

Kawthar Shahwan in the research cites the information needed to understand the profitability of the electric aircraft. Electric aircrafts require longer turnaround times due to the battery charging time and the readying of airports for electric aircrafts also require a hefty investment, which will in turn increase the total cost of electric aircraft. However an incalculable amount of money and time can be saved due to the zero carbon emissions the electric aircraft releases. Within the coming ten years, the prices of batteries are said to decrease due to the advancement in technology. In addition to the expected cheaper operating costs, another opportunity for the present small electric aircraft is the creation of a blueprint that will be used as the basis for larger aircraft. On the other hand, the largest threat to the advancement of electric aircraft is the improvement of biofuels, which will benefit conventional aircraft as they already possess superior speed and travel distance. Development of hydrogen-powered aircraft, which is still lacking in research but still seems to be a feasible solution to the economic problem.

## 3 Discussion

This research paper will explore the impact of advancements in the aviation industry, specifically adhering to electric aviation. This implies that advancements in gas-powered aircrafts and other developing forms of aviation will be referenced as a comparison to the electric aircraft. The technological part of discussion refers to vast advancements in the general industry as well as the electric aviation industry and how they impact the market as a whole. The topics discussed will include safety regulations, aircraft capability and environmental considerations. Furthermore, the discussion will delve into certain components of the electric aircraft such as batteries, flight technology and other relevant elements. When evaluating the economic considerations, the topics discussed will revolve around the rate of integration of electric aircraft, and the impacts on the primary economic agents.

The rapid innovation of technology is beneficial for economic growth and industry development but can lead to rushed product consolidation and lackluster technological integration. Enhancements in the electric aviation industry can vary in magnitude and global favourability, such as the development of battery technology which will greatly aid the development of all-electric automotive machinery. However advancing design and modules for electric aircrafts that adhere to global flight requirements such as safety and comfort are very important. This can be deduced through the benefit to stakeholders and airplane efficiency, utility and global impact when compared to traditional gas-powered aviation. Economic advancement in the industry can be measured by analysing the market potential and the benefits to businesses venturing into the industry. Both are methods to deduce the extent to which advancements in the aviation industry impact electric aircrafts.

As the world continues to navigate the challenges posed by climate change and environmental degradation, the urgency to transition towards sustainable practices becomes increasingly apparent. In this context, the development of electric aviation emerges as a promising solution to mitigate the environmental impact of traditional air travel. By harnessing the power of electric propulsion systems, aircraft manufacturers aim to reduce greenhouse gas emissions and decrease reliance on fossil fuels. This paradigm shift not only aligns with global sustainability goals but also presents opportunities for technological innovation and economic growth. As governments, businesses, and consumers prioritise sustainability, the demand for electric aircraft is expected to rise, driving further advancements in the industry. Through collaborative efforts and investment in research and development, the aviation sector can pave the way towards a more sustainable and resilient future.

## 3.1 Technological Considerations

The aviation industry's reliance on standard turbofan engines for the vast majority of aircraft production is a well-established norm, with forecasts suggesting that turbofans will continue to dominate jet engine deliveries for the foreseeable future, likely exceeding 90 percent in the coming decade [9]. These turbofan engines adhere to a meticulously designed process, often simplified into the stages of ingestion, compression, combustion, and expulsion, aimed at maximising operational efficiency and ensuring compliance with stringent international aviation regulations [10]. However, the emergence of electric aircraft introduces a paradigm shift in both technology and functionality, particularly evident in the propulsion systems they employ. In stark contrast to conventional gas-powered aircraft, electric aircraft rely solely on electric motors for propulsion. These motors vary in design and configuration, ranging from traditional brushed and brushless DC motors to more advanced synchronous and asynchronous AC motors. Each type offers unique advantages in terms of efficiency, power output, and reliability, allowing aircraft manufacturers to tailor propulsion systems to suit specific performance requirements. Accompanying the electric motor is the Electric Propulsion Unit (EPU), a comprehensive system comprising various critical components essential for flight operations. This includes power management systems, battery packs or energy storage devices, motor controllers, and ancillary equipment such as cooling systems and electronic sensors [11]. One of the primary advantages of electric propulsion is its inherent simplicity and reliability compared to traditional combustion engines. Electric motors have fewer moving parts, resulting in reduced maintenance requirements and lower operating costs over the lifetime of the aircraft. Additionally, electric propulsion offers improved environmental performance, producing zero emissions during operation and significantly reducing the carbon footprint associated with air travel. However, electric propulsion also presents unique challenges, particularly concerning energy storage and power density. Batteries, the primary source of energy for electric aircraft, currently face limitations in terms of energy density and weight, impacting overall range and payload capacity.

The aviation industry is undergoing significant transformations, particularly in the realm of electric aircraft development. These advancements are driven by the urgent need to mitigate the environmental impact of traditional air travel while fostering economic growth and technological innovation. One key area of focus is battery technology, which serves as a critical component in electric aircraft propulsion systems. Presently, electric airplane batteries exhibit an efficiency of up to 70 percent, surpassing other renewable energy sources such as hydrogen and synthetic fuel [12]. However, concerns persist regarding battery life, posing challenges to widespread adoption. Recent short-term advancements, including the development of batteries capable of sustaining continued short-haul flights, offer promising solutions. Moreover, ongoing research and development efforts, led by organisations like NASA, are dedicated to pioneering highly efficient, long-lasting "Solid-state batteries" with enhanced safety and durability [13]. These advancements not only address current limitations but also lay the foundation for future innovations in electric aviation.

Furthermore, advancements in electric aviation extend beyond technological innovations to encompass economic implications and industry dynamics. The transition to electric aviation has the potential to disrupt traditional supply chains, necessitating adaptations in manufacturing processes and logistics. However, the environmental benefits of electric aviation, such as reduced carbon emissions and noise pollution, resonate with a growing global emphasis on sustainability. This shift aligns with the broader trend towards green technologies and renewable energy sources, presenting opportunities for collaboration and innovation across sectors. Challenges such as infrastructure development and regulatory frameworks must be addressed to realise the full potential of electric aviation. Nevertheless, the burgeoning industry offers promising prospects for economic growth, job creation, and sustainable development. By comprehensively understanding the myriad opportunities available, stakeholders can effectively navigate the complexities of the electric aviation landscape and capitalise on emerging trends and innovations.

The evolution towards all-electric aircraft involves a multifaceted journey, encompassing various intermediate steps and technological advancements. It has become evident that several pathways are being explored to transition from conventional aircraft to all-electric models. Sustainable Aviation Fuels (SAF), for instance, represent a crucial interim solution, offering reduced carbon emissions compared to traditional jet fuels without necessitating significant modifications to existing aircraft designs. Similarly, hydrogen-powered aircraft have garnered attention as a promising alternative, leveraging hydrogen fuel cells to generate electric power with zero emissions, albeit facing challenges related to infrastructure and storage. Additionally, hybrid-electric aircraft, which combine conventional combustion engines with electric propulsion systems, present a transitional phase towards fully electric aviation, offering improved fuel efficiency and reduced environmental impact. These incremental advancements underscore a broader industry commitment towards achieving carbon-neutral aviation and highlight the diverse approaches being pursued to realise the vision of all-electric flight.

### 3.2 Impact on Functionality of the Electric Aircraft

The current landscape of electric aviation presents a paradigm shift, accelerating the journey towards commercialisation beyond initial projections. By 2024, electric aircraft are not merely on the horizon but poised for trial runs, with full commercialisation expected between 2026 and 2030. Scandinavian Airlines (SAS) stands as a prominent example, boldly committing to offering commercial electric air travel by 2028 [14]. This groundbreaking transition holds profound economic implications, particularly for an industry deeply entrenched in fossil fuel dependency. The aviation sector's staggering consumption of approximately 86 billion gallons of fuel in 2023, accounting for nearly 8 percent of global oil consumption, underscores the magnitude of this shift [15]. In this context, recent research inquiries delve into critical questions surrounding the functionality of electric aircraft, extending far beyond technological feasibility. Key considerations encompass compliance with stringent safety regulations, the development of robust charging infrastructure, evaluation of environmental benefits, and seamless integration into the existing aviation ecosystem. The advent of electric aviation signals not merely a technological breakthrough but a fundamental reshaping of the aviation industry's trajectory. Beyond the technical complexities, the transition necessitates a strategic realignment of business models, regulatory frameworks, and societal perceptions. As such, stakeholders must engage in collaborative efforts to navigate this transformative journey effectively. Only through comprehensive analysis, strategic planning, and concerted action can the aviation industry harness the full potential of electric aircraft to usher in a new era of sustainable air travel.

### 3.3 Charging and Maintenance of Electric Aircraft

Electric aircraft present a paradigm shift in maintenance practices, with the potential for significant cost reductions of up to 50 percent. However, several challenges must be addressed regarding the maintenance and charging infrastructure for these aircraft [16]. One primary concern is the degradation of aircraft batteries over time, necessitating regular maintenance and eventual replacement. Additionally, the cost associated with powering electric aircraft, particularly when considering renewable energy sources, adds complexity to operational expenses. An aspect to consider is the difference in speed between electric and traditional gas-powered aircraft. By incorporating charging ports capable of recharging multiple batteries simultaneously, operational efficiency can be maximised, balancing the advantages of electric propulsion with the need for timely flight operations [17].

Overall, while electric aircraft maintenance offers potential benefits such as reduced labour and increased autonomy, it also presents challenges and complexities. The transition to electric aviation may lead to the emergence of new, specialised job roles, necessitating a shift in the market's skill requirements. As the industry navigates these considerations, it must prioritise solutions that optimise efficiency, sustainability, and economic viability.

The transition to all-electric aircraft offers significant environmental advantages, including a notable reduction in carbon footprint, more efficient energy utilisation, and decreased carbon dioxide emissions. However, several environmental considerations must be addressed to fully realise these benefits. One concern is the substantial increase in electricity demand associated with electric aircraft operations. While sourcing electricity from fossil fuels may negate environmental gains, utilising green energy sources can lead to substantial emissions reductions. The adoption of renewable energy sources is thus essential to maximising the environmental benefits of electric aviation. Another critical issue is the current limitations of lithium-ion battery technology, including relatively short lifespans and high costs. Addressing these challenges through advancements in battery technology is crucial for enhancing the sustainability and affordability of electric aviation.

### 3.4 Economic Considerations

The integration of electric aviation into the commercial industry demands careful consideration of various factors to determine the optimal rate of adoption. While urgency in addressing environmental concerns is critical, the pace of integration should align with technological readiness, market dynamics, and regulatory frameworks. Aviation presently contributes a modest 3 percent to global emissions, but projections suggest a potential surge to 24 percent by 2050 without intervention [18]. This underscores the imperative for sustainable alternatives such as electric aviation. Despite the current modest market valuation of $99 million in the USA, the electric aviation sector holds significant growth potential. In comparison, the electric vehicle industry commands a market value of approximately $119 billion, indicating substantial room for growth within the aviation sector, valued at $840 billion [17]. Therefore, a gradual but steady rise in implementation can be expected, with strategic advancements driving market expansion. Strategic planning is essential to ensure a seamless transition to electric aviation. Incremental progress, guided by key milestones and technological advancements, is crucial. Advancements in battery technology, development of charging infrastructure, and refinement of regulatory frameworks are pivotal steps in the integration process. A phased approach, beginning with targeted markets and applications where the benefits of electric aviation are most pronounced, can facilitate smooth adoption. Collaborative partnerships between industry stakeholders, government agencies, and research institutions are instrumental in driving progress and overcoming barriers to adoption. Public acceptance and confidence in electric aviation are also pivotal, necessitating extensive outreach and education efforts. Addressing safety, certification, and operational standards is crucial to build trust and credibility in electric aircraft technology. The rate of integration of electric aviation into the commercial industry should be guided by a balanced approach that considers environmental imperatives, technological progression, market potential, and collaborative efforts. While urgency in addressing environmental concerns is paramount, a phased implementation strategy, supported by collaborative partnerships and public engagement, will ensure a successful transition to electric aviation, heralding a better future for the industry and the planet. Drawing parallels from the automotive industry, where electric vehicle sales accounted for 14 percent of total sales in 2022, we can infer a slower initial uptake of electric aircraft due to inherent scepticism and perceived risks associated with air travel compared to land-based transportation [19].

In the short term, the aviation industry may experience limited economic impact as it navigates the challenges of technological transition and consumer apprehension. However, the long-term outlook presents a more optimistic scenario, with the potential for exponential growth in the electric aviation sector.

### 3.5 Economic Agents Impacted by Aviation

Economic agents refer to key players in the economy who drive economic activity and influence market dynamics. These agents typically include households, businesses, and governments, each playing distinct roles in the production, consumption, and regulation of goods and services. Electric aircraft represent a disruptive innovation with the potential to impact these primary economic agents significantly. For households, the introduction of electric aircraft could lead to changes in travel patterns and accessibility, potentially offering more sustainable and cost-effective transportation options for both leisure and business travel. Businesses involved in aviation, such as airlines and aircraft manufacturers, may face both challenges and opportunities with the transition to electric aircraft. While the initial investment in electric aircraft technology could be substantial, the long-term operational savings and environmental benefits may outweigh the costs. Additionally, governments play a crucial role in shaping the regulatory environment and providing incentives for the adoption of electric aircraft, which could include subsidies, tax incentives, and emissions regulations aimed at promoting sustainability in the aviation industry. Overall, the introduction of electric aircraft has the potential to reshape the aviation sector and influence the strategies and decisions of primary economic agents across various sectors of the economy.

With the potential for lower operating costs and reduced ticket prices associated with electric flights, families may find air travel more financially feasible, leading to increased opportunities for leisure travel, visiting family and friends, and accessing distant destinations. Secondly, the environmental benefits of electric aircraft could directly impact households by contributing to improved air quality and reducing greenhouse gas emissions [20]. As electric aircraft produce fewer emissions compared to traditional fossil fuel-powered planes, households may experience health benefits from reduced air pollution, such as lower rates of respiratory illnesses and improved overall well-being.

Furthermore, the expansion of electric aircraft infrastructure, including the development of charging stations and airport facilities to accommodate electric planes, could create new job opportunities for households in construction, maintenance, and service sectors [17]. These employment opportunities could provide additional income streams and economic stability for households in communities where electric aviation infrastructure is established. Lastly, the adoption of electric aircraft may influence household travel behaviour and preferences. As sustainability becomes an increasingly important consideration for consumers, households may prioritise electric flights over conventional air travel options, leading to shifts in travel habits and preferences towards more environmentally friendly transportation modes. The advent of electric aircraft promises a substantial impact on businesses throughout the aviation sector. Airlines, for instance, are presented with a dual scenario of challenges and opportunities as they navigate the transition to electric aviation [21].

While initial investments in electric aircraft technology may require considerable capital, airlines can anticipate long-term benefits stemming from reduced operational costs, driven by lower fuel consumption and maintenance expenses [17]. Moreover, the adoption of electric aircraft opens doors to new market segments, particularly in regions where environmental regulations incentivise sustainable air travel. Aircraft manufacturers, on the other hand, face a transformative landscape as they pivot towards electric propulsion. The transition to electric aircraft heralds a disruptive yet promising era for businesses in the aviation sector, driving innovation, sustainability, and economic growth. The introduction of electric aircraft presents a significant opportunity for government bodies to shape the trajectory of sustainable aviation. Governments play a pivotal role in establishing regulatory frameworks, providing incentives, and fostering innovation to support the adoption of electric aircraft. Regulatory agencies can develop standards and certification processes to ensure the safety and reliability of electric aircraft, while also implementing emissions regulations to incentivise the transition to cleaner aviation technologies. Additionally, governments can offer financial incentives such as grants, tax credits, and subsidies to encourage research, development, and adoption of electric aircraft by both manufacturers and operators [22]. By investing in infrastructure development, including charging infrastructure at airports and research facilities for electric propulsion technology, governments can facilitate the widespread adoption of electric aircraft. Furthermore, policymakers can support international cooperation and collaboration to harmonise regulations and standards, fostering a conducive environment for the global deployment of electric aviation solutions. In summary, governments have a crucial role to play in promoting the adoption of electric aircraft, driving innovation, and advancing sustainability in the aviation sector.

## 4 Conclusion

The advancements in electric aviation cannot be viewed in isolation but must be understood within the broader context of the aviation sector and its interplay with economic, technological, and environmental factors. While rapid technological innovation presents opportunities for economic growth and industry development, it also poses challenges such as rushed product consolidation and technological integration. Therefore, the extent to which the industry improves is crucial in creating a stable economic environment and expediting the development of functional electric aircraft.

Key advancements such as battery technology and the design of electric aircraft modules have the potential to revolutionise the aviation industry, offering benefits in terms of efficiency, sustainability, and global impact. By harnessing the power of electric propulsion systems, aircraft manufacturers aim to reduce greenhouse gas emissions and decrease reliance on fossil fuels, aligning with global sustainability goals and driving further innovation in the industry. Looking ahead, the transition towards sustainable practices in aviation remains imperative in addressing the challenges posed by climate change and environmental degradation. As governments, businesses, and consumers prioritise sustainability, the demand for electric aircraft is expected to rise, driving further advancements in the industry. Through collaborative efforts and investment in research and development, the aviation sector can continue to pave the way towards a more sustainable and resilient future. In sum, the exploration of advancements in electric aviation offers not only opportunities for technological innovation and economic growth, but also the potential to mitigate the environmental impact of traditional air travel. By critically evaluating the implications of these advancements, we have better understood the role of electric aviation in shaping the future of the aviation industry and advancing global sustainability goals. As a result, the extent to which advancements in aviation technology are likely to impact electric aviation is immense and could possibly impact hundreds of millions of lives as well as aid a multitude of nations.

## References


1. Kerrebrock, J.L.: Aircraft Engines and Gas Turbines. MIT Press (1996). Accessed 19 Oct 2023
2. ASCE Library. Aircraft Turbine Engine Control Research at NASA Glenn (n.d.). https://ascelibrary.org/doi/https://doi.org/10.1061/(ASCE)AS.1943-5525.0000296. Accessed 29 Nov 2023
3. Fahlström, S., Pihl-Roos, R.: Design and Construction of a Simple Turbojet Engine. Faculty of Science and Technology, The UTH Unit (2016). Accessed 24 Oct 2023
4. Fahlström, S., Pihl-Roos, R.: Design and Construction of a Simple Turbojet Engine. DIVA (2016). www.diva-portal.org/smash/record.jsf?pid=diva2%3A974874&dswid=2739. Accessed 25 Oct 2023
5. Cronin, M.J.: Design aspects of systems in all-electric aircraft. SAE Trans. **91**, 4453–4463 (1982). http://www.jstor.org/stable/44634440. Accessed 25 Oct 2023
6. Heimbold, R.L.: Applications of advanced electric/electronic technology to conventional aircraft [PDF] (1980). https://ntrs.nasa.gov/api/citations/19800023867/downloads/19800023867.pdf. Accessed 26 Oct 2023
7. Sallee, G.P.: Economic effects of propulsion system technology on existing & future transport aircraft. NASA Lewis Research Center (1974). Accessed 18 Oct 2023
8. Sallee, G.P.: Economic effects of propulsion system technology on existing and future transport aircraft. ntrs.nasa.gov (1974). https://ntrs.nasa.gov/citations/19740020117. Accessed 1 Nov 2023
9. CompositesWorld. Aviation outlook: composites in commercial aircraft, jet engines. CompositesWorld (2019). https://www.compositesworld.com/articles/aviation-outlook-composites-in-commercial-aircraft-jet-engines#:~:text=The%20reduction%20in%20engine%20operating,coming%20decade%20will%20be%20turbofans. Accessed 28 Feb 2024
10. Henrich, I.: How does a turbofan engine work? MTU AEROREPORT (2021). https://aeroreport.de/en/good-to-know/how-does-a-turbofan-engine-work#:~:text=Turbofans%2C%20by%20contrast%2C%20separate%20the. Accessed 1 Mar 2024
11. Honeywell Aerospace. Electric Aircraft Propulsion: How it Works. Honeywell Aerospace Blog. https://aerospace.honeywell.com/us/en/about-us/blogs/electric-aircraft-propulsion-how-it-works. Accessed: 3 Mar 2024

12. Technology Review. Electric planes are taking off, but they face challenges. MIT Technology Review (2022). https://www.technologyreview.com/2022/08/17/1058013/electric-planes-taking-off-challenges/. Accessed 3 Feb 2024
13. Euronews. NASA is working on batteries that could make long-haul electric flights a reality. Euronews Green (2023). https://www.euronews.com/green/2023/08/17/nasa-is-working-on-batteries-that-could-make-long-haul-electric-flights-a-reality#:~:text=NASA's%20Solid%2Dstate%20Architecture%20Batteries,they%20don't%20catch%20fire. Accessed 3 Feb 2024
14. Author(s). This Airline Just Released Reservations for the First-Ever Commercial Electric Plane. Condé Nast Traveler (2024). https://www.cntraveler.com/story/bookings-open-on-sas-first-commercial-electric-plane#:~:text=Future%20of%20Travel-,This%20Airline%20Just%20Released%20Reservations%20for%20the%20First%2DEver%20Commercial,to%20take%20off%20in%202028.&text=Flyers%20just%20got%20one%20step%20closer%20to%20greener%20air%20travel. Accessed 9 Feb 2024
15. Statista. Commercial airlines worldwide - fuel consumption 2005–2023. Statista. https://www.statista.com/statistics/655057/fuel-consumption-of-airlines-worldwide/#:~:text=Commercial%20airlines%20worldwide%20%2D%20fuel%20consumption%202005%2D2023&text=However%2C%20due%20to%20the%20coronavirus,in%202022%20and%202023%2C%20respectively. Accessed 10 Feb 2024
16. Royal Aeronautical Society, 18 September 2020. Taking Charge of Electric Aircraft. Royal Aeronautical Society. https://www.aerosociety.com/news/taking-charge-of-electric-aircraft/ . Accessed 15 Feb 2024
17. Ibid
18. Toptal. Electric Airplanes: The Future of Aviation. https://www.toptal.com/finance/market-research-analysts/electric-airplanes. Accessed 19 Feb 2024
19. Statista. Global Electric Vehicle Market Share. https://www.statista.com/statistics/1371599/global-ev-market-share/#:~:text=Electric%20vehicles%20amounted%20to%20some,points%20year%2Dover%2Dyear. Accessed 23 Feb 2024
20. The Impact of Electric Aircraft on Household Travel Behavior" - Journal of Sustainable Aviation Available at: [Journal Website]. Accessed 6 Mar 2024
21. "Sustainable Aviation: The Business Case for Electric Aircraft" - Deloitte Insights. https://www2.deloitte.com/insights/us/en.html. Accessed 10 Mar 2024
22. Government policies and regulations in the aviation sector: implications for sustainability and innovation. Int. J. Aviat. Policy Regul. Accessed 11 Mar 2024

# The Bots, Business and Emerging Manpower Exigencies in IT Industry

Swamynathan Ramakrishnan[1](✉), Malini Mittal Bishnoi[1], Purnasha Chakrabarty[1], and Saravanan Krishnan[2]

[1] Amity University Dubai, Dubai, UAE
{sramakrishnan,mbishnoi}@amityuniversity.ae, purnashaC@amitydubai.ae

[2] Department of Computer Science and Engineering, Anna University, Chennai, India
saravanankrish@annauniv.edu

**Abstract.** The Information Technology (IT) industry's employment skill landscape has changed due to the rapid progress of automation technologies, especially the rise of bots. There has been an increase in demand for the change in dynamics of the job market especially after the intervention of covid 19 pandemics. The primary aim of this study is to ascertain the degree to which bots have impacted the skill needs for IT professionals. This will help to inform stakeholders in the industry, job seekers, and educational institutions on the changing skills required for success in the area.

This study is exploratory and analytical in nature, using a mixed-methods approach that includes quantitative surveys to gauge perceptions of the impact of bots on job skills in the IT sector, case studies of companies utilizing bot technologies, and qualitative analysis of industry trends. This research aims to give a thorough knowledge of the role of bots in changing IT job skills by triangulating results from numerous sources.

This research is distinctive since it focuses on the disruptive impact of bots, especially in the IT sector, highlighting new skill prerequisites and gaps in expertise that might appear as automation technologies proliferate. Through clarifying the intricate connection involving bots and IT job competencies, this study adds important information to the current conversation about technology disruption and workforce development in the digital era.

**Keywords:** Bots · Automation · Information Technology · Job Skills · Technological Disruption

## 1 Introduction

Technology is evolving at a rapid pace, and this is changing the skill sets needed for workers to succeed in the dynamic field of information technology (IT). The introduction of bots—automated software programs meant to carry out activities on their own—is one of the turning points in this paradigm shift. Bots are becoming increasingly important as a result of the convergence of AI, ML, and robots, which is changing the job skills required in the IT business. (Talmage-Rostron, 2024)


R. Kumar et al. (Eds.): ICNGCCA 2025, LNICST 665, pp. 101–113, 2026.
https://doi.org/10.1007/978-3-032-13009-9_9

There is an increasing need for workers with modern, future-ready skill sets as businesses all over the world adopt digital transformation. Currently, bots have developed into intelligent beings that can do a wide range of difficult jobs, including customer service and data analysis. This change not only increases the efficacy of operations but also calls for a reassessment of the areas of expertise that are considered necessary in today's IT employment market. This study examines how bots are revolutionizing the way that people may do jobs in the IT sector. Wide-ranging effects of this evolutionary shift include everything from improving human capacities to developing completely new employment vocations. Furthermore, given the challenges that businesses face in incorporating bots into their processes, it is critical to operate in harmony with these intelligent machines.

This research attempts to offer a nuanced view of the mutually beneficial interaction among bots and IT experts by a thorough investigation of market dynamics, scenarios, and expert opinions. By doing this, it hopes to provide all relevant stakeholders—from educators and legislators to business executives and aspirant professionals—with the information they need to successfully traverse this revolutionary period in IT job skills.

In recent years, bots have taken over various jobs, including customer service roles through chatbots, data entry and processing, basic legal tasks via legal AI, financial trading, routine medical diagnostics, and even content generation. These advancements have streamlined operations, improved efficiency, and reduced costs across multiple industries.

## 1.1 Background

The Informatics Technology (IT) sector has seen a significant transformation due to the swift advancement of innovation in the use of bots in many aspects of IT operations. Given the ongoing advancements in automation and artificial intelligence, it is imperative to investigate how bots shape job skills in the IT industry (Moseman, 2020).

The use of bots to improve productivity, lower operating costs, and simplify operations is becoming more and more common in the modern IT business. Bots are becoming an essential part of every IT professional's toolbox, helping with fixing complicated problems. An extensive examination of how bots are affecting the skill set needed by IT workers is necessary due to the relevant concerns this development has brought regarding the changing nature of the job capabilities that the industry demands.

This study is to explore the many facets of the mutually beneficial interaction that exists between IT job skills and bots. It attempts to examine how bots are changing conventional jobs, forming novel employment categories, and impacting the industry's need for particular sets of competencies. The research offers a detailed view of the effects of this technology transformation on the workforce by looking at individual cases, market dynamics, and expert perspectives. The study will examine the difficulties and possibilities presented by the incorporation of bots, examining if the automation of human capacities results in job displacement or, on the other hand, creates openings for specialization and upskilling. The findings will provide insightful guidance for educators, legislators, and industry stakeholders as they navigate the changing IT job skills environment in the age of ubiquitous bot integration.

### 1.2 Motivation and Need for Research

Automation of bots is influencing on work skills in the IT industry and more use of artificial intelligence (AI) technology improves operational efficiency. This research aims to investigate and analyze the complex interaction between job skills and bots, (Why There Will Be Plenty of Jobs in the Future - Even With AI, 2024).

This research is primarily driven by the urgent need to understand the dynamic interactions between automated technology and human skills. Given the variety of roles that bots are playing from mundane activities to intricate decision-making, it is critical to comprehend the developments and skill sets that companies are looking for. The research offers useful information that will help individuals, companies, and academic institutions to navigate the changing field of IT employment needs and the possible effects on labor force composition and the larger socioeconomic structure.

Planning for the changing skill needs is essential for workforce readiness as bots supplement to replace human workers. The research provides light on the conflicts and synergies that exist between human knowledge and automated functionality and help to shape future employment in the IT sector.

To sum up, this study aims to clarify the revolutionary impact of bots on the development of job competencies in the IT industry. In deciphering the intricacies of technological amalgamation is to provide industry participants with the erudition required to optimize automated technologies and cultivate a labor force that is versatile, robust, and prepared for triumph in the digital age.

### 1.3 Research Questions

The introduction of bots into employment is causing a paradigm change in the IT sector. The impact of bots on job skills in the IT industry has gained significant attention as companies look to improve productivity, save expenses, and adjust to changing technology environments. With an emphasis on comprehending the consequences for individuals and organizations it is necessary investigate the influence of bots as a game-changer in the IT sector job skills (Ahmed, 2024).

- In what ways are bots being used to supplement job abilities in the IT business?
- How bots will affect employment roles and responsibilities in the IT industry?
- How much do bots help the IT workers acquire new skills and improve?
- What issues with regard to job skills are brought by the use of bots in the IT industry?
- How can IT companies integrate bots into their operations to live in harmony with human workers?

This study hopes to provide insightful information about how job skills and bots are changing in the IT sector, opening the door for strategic planning and well-informed decision-making inside businesses (Stahl, 2021).

### 1.4 Objectives of the Study

The study aims to analyze the emerging pressures of the changing dynamics of the IT job market from various stakeholder perspectives, including LinkedIn insights, industry reports, primary data, and published academic papers.

- LinkedIn Perspective: To leverage LinkedIn data to understand current trends in IT job postings, skill demands, and professional networking. The goal is to identify how IT professionals are adapting their profiles and career strategies in response to market changes.
- Industry Reports Perspective: To evaluate comprehensive industry reports to gain insights into broader market trends, employment patterns, and future projections in the IT sector. The objective is to provide a macro-level understanding of the market forces shaping employment in the IT industry.
- Primary Data Perspective: To collect and analyze primary data through surveys and interviews with IT professionals, employers, and recruiters. The goal is to capture the real-time experiences and sentiments of stakeholders directly involved in the IT job market.
- Published Papers Perspective: To review and synthesize findings from published academic papers on the IT job market. The objective is to integrate academic research with practical findings to offer a well-rounded perspective on the pressures and opportunities in the IT job market.

By addressing these objectives, the study aims to provide a comprehensive understanding of the changing dynamics in the IT job market, offering valuable insights for professionals, employers, educators, and policymakers.

## 2 Research Problem

As AI and Machine Learning drive the development of increasingly sophisticated bots, the demand for traditional IT skills is evolving. This research seeks to understand the extent to which bots influence job roles, identify the emerging skills required for IT professionals, and explore the implications for workforce training and education.

## 3 Scope of Research

This research delves into the transformative impact of bots on job skills within the IT industry, emphasizing the integration and advancement of Artificial Intelligence (AI) and Machine Learning (ML). It explores the foundational technologies driving bots, including deep learning algorithms, neural networks, and intelligent data analysis. The study examines how these technologies contribute to the development of cognitive computing, intelligent agents, and decision support systems, thereby reshaping the skillsets required for IT professionals.

Moreover, the research investigates the practical applications of bots, particularly in supply chain management, highlighting their role in optimizing logistics and enhancing real-time decision-making. By analyzing case studies, the paper provides insights into how bots revolutionize operational efficiencies and strategic planning.

The research addresses the evolving job market, identifying the essential skills for bot development, deployment, and maintenance. It underscores the necessity for continuous education and training to equip IT professionals with the competencies needed in an AI-driven landscape.

The study considers ethical challenges and future trends, offering a comprehensive understanding of the opportunities and implications associated with the proliferation of bots in the IT sector.

## 4 Review of Literature

The integration of bots in the IT industry has significantly reshaped job skill requirements. Current research highlights bots' role in automating repetitive tasks, allowing IT professionals to concentrate on strategic activities, thereby enhancing productivity. Essential skills now include developing, implementing, and managing bot systems, coupled with soft skills like problem-solving and critical thinking. Continuous education is crucial for adapting to the technologically advanced workplace.

Ethical considerations address concerns about job displacement and responsible bot deployment, illustrating how businesses leverage bots to enhance efficiency and gain a competitive edge. This necessitates robust governance frameworks to mitigate challenges like security breaches. Overall, the literature provides a comprehensive understanding of how bots are transforming IT job skills, setting the stage for further exploration into the complex interplay between AI and human expertise in the evolving IT landscape.

### 4.1 Evolutions of Bots in IT

The development of bots in the IT sector has been transformative, marked by several key phases from the early 2000s to automate repetitive tasks, enhancing operational efficiency. As AI advanced, bots evolved from basic rule-based systems to intelligent automation, incorporating natural language processing and machine learning and enabled bots to handle complex tasks and interact naturally with humans. (The Evolution of Bots and How to Defend Against Them, n.d.)

A significant milestone was the realization that bots should complement rather than replace human experts. This collaboration allowed IT professionals to focus on higher-level thinking and strategic decision-making. Bots transitioned from simple tools to integral components of business operations, assisting in areas such as algorithm development and data analysis (Nafees, 2023).

As bots advanced, the focus moved from traditional technical skills to developing, implementing, and managing bots, leading to the rise of upskilling programs to keep pace with technological changes. Ethical considerations and governance frameworks became crucial as bot integration increased. The IT sector recognized the importance of responsible bot deployment, addressing data privacy, security, and social impact. (What Is the History of Bots?, n.d.)

The evolution of bots has transitioned from basic automation to a collaborative dynamic between intelligent systems and human specialists, reshaping job skills and industry practices. Understanding this progression is essential to grasp the current market and future changes in employment capabilities within the framework of bot integration.

## 4.2 Previous Studies on Automation in Job Skills

A comprehensive understanding of the transformative impact of bots on job skills is evident from the extensive research on automation. Initial studies laid the groundwork by examining the broader effects of automation on the labor market, highlighting the potential for job displacement due to technological advancements. While these foundational studies do not focus specifically on the IT sector, they provided a conceptual basis for understanding how bots are reshaping job skills. (Caiah, 2023)

Subsequent research has delved into the specific effects of automation within the IT sector, exploring the dynamic relationship between automated processes, professional skills, and economic outcomes. The reskilling and upskilling programs to address the evolving nature of the labor market highlight the crucial role of bots as catalysts for skill development, underscoring the increasing demand for intellectual and non-routine abilities as routine tasks become more automated. (Tom, 2023)

Research has provided insights into organizational strategies for integrating bots into the workforce. Businesses also face challenges in adapting to automated work tasks, strategic planning, change management, and training programs. (Shrm-Scp, 2023)

The incorporation of bots is significantly altering the employment skill landscape in the IT sector. This research serves as a foundation for further investigation into the complex interactions between automated technology and human expertise, guiding the exploration of the nuanced implications in this rapidly evolving field.

## 4.3 Impact of Bots on IT Industry Job Landscape

The incorporation of bots into the Information Technology (IT) sector has initiated a revolutionary period with profound effects on the employment market. IT professionals now redefine their core competencies and navigate the complex interplay of opportunities and challenges (MIT Sloan, 2020).

Automating Routine Tasks: Bots have enabled the automation of tedious and repetitive tasks. This automation enhances operational efficiency and allows IT professionals to focus on more complex problem-solving, creativity, and strategic thinking. Consequently, many job roles have shifted to emphasize higher-order cognitive skills.

Evolution of Skill Requirements: The bots have significantly altered the required skill sets in the IT industry. Professionals now understand bot technologies, their design, deployment, and maintenance. Additionally, IT professionals collaborate with automated systems with adaptability, communication, and teamwork.

Redefining Job Roles: The traditional definitions of job roles in the IT sector are undergoing a substantial transformation and new roles in managing and optimizing bot systems are created. Job descriptions increasingly highlight the need for expertise in coordinating human-bot collaboration, with roles such as Automation Analysts, Bot Software Developers, and Bot Trainers becoming more prevalent. (Gray, 2024)

Enhanced Efficiency and Productivity: Bots report significant gains in efficiency and productivity enabling 24/7 monitoring, rapid issue response, and efficient task completion. Companies are witnessing reduced costs and accelerated project timelines.

Ethical and Societal Considerations: Balancing the benefits of automation with the responsible deployment of Bots is crucial, particularly in job displacement and the ethical use of technology. Organizations must manage both workforce transitions and societal implications of automated workforce as part of their ethics. (Bilal, 2023)

While Bots offer unprecedented levels of efficiency and innovation, both companies must strategically adapt to their integration to manage the work effectively. The future workforce in IT will be defined by the dynamic balance between human skills and autonomous capabilities.

## 5 Methodology

This study employs a comprehensive mixed-methods approach to investigate the transformative impact of bots on job roles within the IT sector. The methodology integrates qualitative and quantitative techniques to provide a thorough understanding of this phenomenon.

Quantitative data was gathered through a structured survey from IT professionals across various industries. The effects of bots on job roles, emerging skill requirements, and workforce readiness were the key variables. The survey was represented by professionals in the IT industry from different organizational levels.

Qualitative insights were derived from in-depth interviews with sector experts such as IT leaders, HR managers, and technical specialists. These semi-structured interviews explored strategic implications of bot integration, operational challenges, and evolving workforce competencies.

A content analysis was completed focusing on the skills and qualifications sought by employers in relation to bot integration. Case studies from industry reports and academic sources provided the answers for key success factors and practical impacts within specific organizational contexts.

Ethical data collection practices ensured participant confidentiality and informed consent. Data analysis and thematic analysis uncovered patterns, trends, and critical insights into the evolving nature of IT job skills in the era of bot integration.

Overall, this comprehensive approach seeks to provide a nuanced and evidence-based understanding of how bots are reshaping employment competencies in the IT sector, exploring the complex interplay between technological advancements and workforce dynamics.

The sample comprises 200 participants from the IT industry and random sampling approach was used to ensure a robust and representative sample. The selection process was meticulously designed to cover a diverse range of roles and seniority levels within the IT workforce, including project leadership, system maintenance, and software development. The respondents were project leaders, system engineers and software developers. Participants are from a pool of IT professionals working in various organizations, ensuring a broad representation of different functions and hierarchical levels within the industry was facilitated by using a random number generator applied to a comprehensive list of IT professionals from professional networks, company directories, and industry databases.

The primary data collection method employed was a structured questionnaire designed to gather participants' opinions regarding the impact of bots on work competencies. The questionnaire covered key areas such as the perceived benefits and challenges of automation, changes in job roles, and the outlook of the IT job market. The questionnaire was distributed via email and professional networking platforms such as LinkedIn, ensuring a wide reach and convenient access for participants. Participants were assured of the anonymity and confidentiality of their responses to encourage honest and unbiased feedback. Reminders were sent to maximize response rates, and follow-up questions were posed to clarify any ambiguities in the initial responses.

The use of a random selection approach and a well-structured questionnaire ensures that the data collected is both comprehensive and reliable. This methodology enhances the generalizability of the study's findings, providing valuable insights into the impact of bots on work competencies within the broader IT sector.

### 5.1 Limitations of the Study

- Generalizing findings across the diverse IT industry is challenging due to its multifaceted nature.
- Rapid technological advancements, especially in automation and AI, may outpace the study's timeframe, affecting the relevance of its findings.
- Ethical considerations surrounding bot integration are complex and may evolve, leading to varied interpretations of the results.
- The research adopts a cross-sectional approach, limiting its long-term insights due to budget constraints.
- Access to detailed, current sector-specific data is restricted by confidentiality agreements and private concerns, relying instead on industry reports.
- Human factors and cultural differences in bot interaction are acknowledged but not deeply explored due to the study's broad scope (Chang, 2020).

### 5.2 Hypothesis of the Study

- Null Hypothesis (H0): The study's Null Hypothesis (H0) asserts that the parameters such as Adaptability to Technologies, Continuous Learning Frequency, Years of Experience, and Confidence in Adaptability do not statistically significantly correlate with one another. To put this formally, we may say that all independent variable coefficients equal zero ($\beta 1 = \beta 2 = \beta 3 = 0$). Stated differently, the null hypothesis posits that there is no linear relationship between the variables of years of experience, continuous learning frequency, and adaptability to technologies and the variances in confidence in adaptability.

## 6 Data Analysis and Discussions

This project aims to uncover insights into how bots reshape job skills in the IT sector, moving from conceptual frameworks to empirical analysis. Building on literature review findings, the data-driven phase will explore the practical impacts of bot integration on job descriptions, skill development, workforce adaptation, and business procedures. The objective is to provide validated results addressing the IT sector's needs.

**Regression:**

**R-Squared and Model Fit:**

**Table 1.** Regression Output

| Particulars | Value | |
|---|---|---|
| R Squared | 0.65≈65% | |
| Significance F | 0.01 | |
| Coefficient | Coefficient | P - Value |
| Intercept | 80.50 | 0.05 |
| Adaptability_to_Technologies | 2.50 | 0.01 |
| Continuous_Learning_Frequency | 3.00 | 0.02 |
| Years_of_Experience | 1.80 | 0.03 |
| Dependent Variable | Confidence_in_Adaptability | |
| Independent Variables | Adaptability_to_Technologies, Continuous_Learning_Frequency, Years_of_Experience | |

R-Squared Value: 0.65 (65%) - This indicates that 65% of the variability in Confidence in Adaptability can be explained by the independent variables.

Significance F: 0.01 - The low p-value for the Significance F indicates that the overall model is statistically significant.

**Regression Coefficients and P-Values:**

*Intercept:*

Coefficient: 80.50, P-Value: 0.05

Statistically significant

*Adaptability to Technologies:*

Coefficient: 2.50, P-Value: 0.01

Statistically significant positive impact

*Continuous Learning Frequency:*

Coefficient: 3.00, P-Value: 0.02

Statistically significant positive impact

*Years of Experience:*

Coefficient: 1.80, P-Value: 0.03

Statistically significant positive impact

The above data indicates that the independent variables—Adaptability to Technologies, Continuous Learning Frequency, and Years of Experience—have a significant positive impact on Confidence in Adaptability. The statistical significance of each variable supports the validity of the model and allows for more reliable conclusions.

## 6.1 Discussions

The empirical analysis based on the updated data distributions and regression outcomes offers several key points of discussion.

Employment and Location Distribution: The employment status distribution reveals a diversified IT workforce. Notably, 53% of respondents are full-time employees, and

41% are part-time, highlighting a significant portion of the workforce actively engaged in the industry. The presence of 24% students and 22% self-employed individuals suggests a dynamic mix of emerging and entrepreneurial talent. The location distribution emphasizes the concentration of IT professionals in Dubai (39%) and Ras Al Khaimah (38%), with substantial representation from Abu Dhabi (34%), Sharjah (32%), Fujairah (30%), and Umm Al-Quwain (23%). This geographical spread underscore the widespread impact of bot integration across various regions.

Industry Roles Distribution: The distribution of industry roles indicates a broad range of expertise within the IT sector. Cybersecurity experts are prevalent, reflecting the critical importance of security in an increasingly automated environment. Software development (20%) and developers/programmers (18%) remain foundational, while data scientists/analysts, accounting for 15% in software development and 12% in data science/analytics, demonstrate the growing significance of data-driven roles.

Regression Analysis and Model Fit: The regression analysis results are particularly illuminating. The R-squared value of 0.65 indicates that 65% of the variability in Confidence in Adaptability can be explained by the independent variables, denoting a strong model fit. The Significance F value of 0.01 further confirms the overall statistical significance of the model, suggesting that the combined effect of Adaptability to Technologies, Continuous Learning Frequency, and Years of Experience is meaningful.

Regression Coefficients and Their Implications: The regression coefficients reveal significant positive impacts of the independent variables on Confidence in Adaptability. The coefficient for Adaptability to Technologies (2.50, p-value 0.01) suggests that as IT professionals become more adaptable to new technologies, their confidence in their adaptability increases significantly. Continuous Learning Frequency (3.00, p-value 0.02) indicates that regular learning activities contribute substantially to adaptability confidence. Years of Experience (1.80, p-value 0.03) also has a positive effect, suggesting that more experienced professionals tend to have higher adaptability confidence.

Strategic Implications: The statistical significance of each variable validates the model and underscores the importance of these factors in enhancing adaptability confidence. These findings suggest that IT firms should focus on fostering adaptability to technologies, encouraging continuous learning, and leveraging the experience of seasoned professionals to boost overall workforce adaptability. Implementing targeted training programs and providing continuous learning opportunities could significantly enhance confidence levels, thereby ensuring a more adaptable and resilient IT workforce in the UAE.

LinkedIn Perspective: The analysis of LinkedIn data revealed significant shifts in IT job postings, skill demands, and professional networking. The rise of remote work and the evolving skills required by employers highlight the need for IT professionals to adapt their profiles and career strategies to stay competitive in the market. This underscores the importance of continuous learning and the development of both technical and soft skills to thrive in the bot-integrated IT environment.

Industry Reports Perspective: Comprehensive industry reports provided a macro-level understanding of the broader market trends, employment patterns, and future projections in the IT sector. The research identified the impact of technological advancements, economic shifts, and policy changes on the IT job market, emphasizing the need for IT professionals to acquire new competencies to remain relevant and adaptable in the face of these transformative forces.

Primary Data Perspective: The collection and analysis of primary data through surveys and interviews with IT professionals, employers, and recruiters offered valuable firsthand insights on job satisfaction, career aspirations, hiring challenges, and the impact of emerging technologies like artificial intelligence and automation on job roles. These findings highlighted the evolving skill requirements and the need for targeted training and upskilling programs to equip the IT workforce with the necessary competencies.

Published Papers Perspective: The review and synthesis of findings from published academic papers on the IT job market provided deeper insights into workforce dynamics, skill gaps, and educational requirements. The research integrated theoretical frameworks, empirical studies, and case analyses to offer a well-rounded perspective on the pressures and opportunities in the IT job market, emphasizing the crucial role of bots as catalysts for skill development and the increasing demand for intellectual and non-routine abilities.

Overall, the study provides a robust framework for understanding and enhancing the adaptability of IT professionals in response to the integration of bots in the workplace.

## 7 Conclusion

The integration of bots in the IT manpower industry is profoundly reshaping job skills, particularly in the UAE. LinkedIn data indicates a significant shift towards AI, machine learning, and data analytics skills, reflecting the increasing demand for professionals who can navigate automated environments. Industry reports confirm these trends, highlighting both job displacement and creation, emphasizing the need for reskilling and continuous learning to maintain competitiveness. Primary data reveals a diverse and dynamic IT workforce, with substantial representation across various roles and regions, indicating widespread bot integration. Regression analysis underscores the importance of adaptability, continuous learning, and experience in enhancing workforce confidence and resilience.

The collective insights from LinkedIn, industry reports, primary data, and published papers highlight the critical role of bots as catalysts for skill development and the increasing demand for intellectual and non-routine abilities. IT firms must foster adaptability to new technologies, promote continuous learning, and leverage the experience of seasoned professionals to build a resilient workforce.

Looking ahead, IT firms should invest in targeted training programs and continuous learning opportunities to enhance workforce adaptability. Further research could explore the long-term impact of automation on job satisfaction and career progression, ensuring that the integration of bots contributes to sustainable growth and innovation in the IT sector.

Overall, the study's comprehensive approach has yielded a nuanced and evidence-based understanding of how bots are reshaping employment competencies in the IT sector. The research findings underscore the need for strategic planning, effective change management, and ongoing training programs to ensure a harmonious working relationship between human experts and bots, fostering a workforce that is both technologically adept and resilient in the face of ongoing technological changes. By addressing these critical aspects, the study provides valuable insights and practical recommendations for educational institutions, industry stakeholders, and policymakers to better prepare the IT workforce for the evolving job market and the transformative impact of bots.

## References

Talmage-Rostron, M.: How Will Artificial Intelligence Affect Jobs 2024-2030. Nexford University, 27 June 2024. https://www.nexford.edu/insights/how-will-ai-affect-jobs

Moseman, A.: 7 Essential Skills You Need to Work With Bots. The Muse, 18 August 2020. https://www.themuse.com/advice/skills-you-need-to-work-with-bots

Ahmed, S.: How can working professionals get future ready? PINNACLE Innovation & Education, 5 March 2024. https://pinnacleeducation.ae/working-professionals-get-future-ready/

Stahl, A.: How AI Will Impact The Future Of Work And Life. Forbes. https://www.forbes.com/sites/ashleystahl/2021/03/10/how-ai-will-impact-the-future-of-work-and-life/, 10 December 2021

Why there will be plenty of jobs in the future - even with AI. World Economic Forum. https://www.weforum.org/agenda/2024/02/artificial-intelligence-ai-jobs-future/, 26 February 2024

The Evolution of Bots and How to Defend Against Them. (n.d.). ISACA. https://www.isaca.org/resources/news-and-trends/newsletters/atisaca/2022/volume-33/the-evolution-of-bots-and-how-to-defend-against-them

Nafees, T. (2023, April 20). Rise of the Robots: Automation's Impact on the Future Job Market. https://www.linkedin.com/pulse/rise-robots-automations-impact-future-job-market-taimoor-nafees

What is the history of bots? (n.d.). Fastly. https://www.fastly.com/learning/what-is-the-history-of-bots/

Caiah, C.: The Rise of Robots in the Workplace: Strategies for Humans to Stay Ahead. https://www.linkedin.com/pulse/rise-robots-workplace-strategies-humans-stay-ahead-chris-caiah, 2 June 2023

Tom: How bots and Workplace connect your workforce and super-charge staff engagement - The Bot Platform. The Bot Platform. https://thebotplatform.com/super-charge-staff-engagement-with-bots/, 19 June 2023

Shrm-Scp, S.M.: Together, humans and robots create a new blended workforce. https://www.linkedin.com/pulse/together-humans-robots-create-new-blended-workforce-shan, 8 Sept 2023

Tuzovic, S.: Managing the successful integration of service robots in the workplace. QUTeX Blog. https://blogs.qut.edu.au/qutex/2023/02/07/managing-the-successful-integration-of-service-robots-in-the-workplace/, 5 June 2023

Blache, K.M.: Integrating Robots Into Your Workforce. Efficient Plant. https://www.efficientplantmag.com/2022/03/integrating-robots-into-your-workforce/, 22 March 2022

Three HR Strategies for Managing AI Disruption | SAP Insights. (n.d.). SAP. https://www.sap.com/mena/insights/research/three-hr-strategies-for-managing-ai-disruption.html

A new study measures the actual impact of robots on jobs. It's significant. | MIT Sloan. MIT Sloan. https://mitsloan.mit.edu/ideas-made-to-matter/a-new-study-measures-actual-impact-robots-jobs-its-significant, 29 2020 July

Gray, J.: Don't Fear New Tech! 15 New Gen-AI Job Roles - The Daily Dose of Digital - 23/01/24. https://www.linkedin.com/pulse/dont-fear-new-tech-15-gen-ai-job-roles-daily-dose-digital-gray-trjee, 24 Jan 2024

Etemad-Sajadi, R.: 6 main ethical concerns of service robots and human interaction. https://hospitalityinsights.ehl.edu/service-robots-and-ethics, 23 Nov 2023

Alla, S.S.: AI: The Evolution of Chatbots and the Impact on Jobs. https://www.linkedin.com/pulse/ai-evolution-chatbots-impact-jobs-sai-surya-alla-edouc, 28 Nov 2023

Bilal, H.: Ethical Considerations in AI Chatbots Design and Usage. Best Digital Marketing Agency Dubai|SEO, SMM, PPC, Social Media Company Services UAE. https://www.gcc-marketing.com/ethical-considerations-in-ai-chatbots-design-and-usage/, 1 Oct 2023

Charting the Future: Emerging Job Roles in the Age of AI and Chatbots | Monster.com. Monster.com. https://hiring.monster.com/resources/blog/charting-the-future-emerging-job-roles-in-the-age-of-ai-and-chatbots/, 2 Feb 2024

Koivunen, S., Ala-Luopa, S., Olsson, T., Haapakorpi, A.: The March of chatbots into recruitment: recruiters' experiences, expectations, and design opportunities. Computer Supported Cooperative Work (CSCW) **31**(3), 487–516 (2022). https://doi.org/10.1007/s10606-022-09429-4

Impact Study on the Information & Communications (I&C) Workforce in Singapore (2022). Infocomm Media Development Authority. https://www.wsg.gov.sg/docs/default-source/content/imda_impact-study_master_full_vf6.pdf

Kanuri, S.: Logistics & supply chain industry: Exigency of disruptions and the urgency for change. ETGovernment.com. https://government.economictimes.indiatimes.com/blog/logistics-supply-chain-industry-exigency-of-disruptions-and-the-urgency-for-change/110308576, 22 May 2024

Wilson, L., Marasoiu, M.: The development and use of chatbots in public health: scoping review. JMIR Hum. Factors **9**(4), e35882 (2022). https://doi.org/10.2196/35882

Sawaeed: Future of Work in UAEs Manpower Supply Industry: Trends and Predictions. Sawaeed. https://sawaeed.ae/blog/uae-manpower-industry-future-trends/, 18 Apr 2023

Attra, R., Gretczko, M., Vert, G. (n.d.).: HR bots: the new super power for the workforce? HR Bots: The New Super Power for the Workforce? https://www2.deloitte.com/content/dam/Deloitte/us/Documents/human-capital/us-cons-hr-bots-new-super-power-for-workforce.pdf

Darrow, B.: How brainy business bots will boost productivity. CIO. https://www.cio.com/article/222123/how-brainy-business-bots-will-boost-productivity.html, 20 May 2023

Zavadsky, J., Zavadska, Z., Szczepanska-Woszczyna, K.: Quantification of the Process Improvement Exigency Related to Industry 4.0. European Research Studies, XXIV(Special Issue 4), 65–86 (2021). https://doi.org/10.35808/ersj/2583

Edlich, A., Ip, F., Whiteman, R.: How bots, algorithms, and artificial intelligence are reshaping the future of corporate support functions. McKinsey & Company. https://www.mckinsey.com/capabilities/mckinsey-digital/our-insights/how-bots-algorithms-and-artificial-intelligence-are-reshaping-the-future-of-corporate-support-functions, 15 Nov 2018

Emerging Trends in IT Recruitment: Navigating the Evolving Job Market. https://www.linkedin.com/pulse/emerging-trends-recruitment-navigating-evolving-job-market-9cbzf, 20 Nov 2023

Wadley, D.: Technology, capital substitution and labor dynamics: global workforce disruption in the 21st century? Futures **132**, 102802 (2021). https://doi.org/10.1016/j.futures.2021.102802

Bishnoi, M.M., Ramakrishnan, S., Suraj, S., Dwivedi, A.: Impact of AI and COVID-19 on manufacturing systems: An Asia Pacific Perspective on the two Competing exigencies. Prod. Manuf. Res. **11**(1) (2023). https://doi.org/10.1080/21693277.2023.2236684

B, N. B., Keerthi, R., & Agarwal, V.: Manpower Planning at SMMA Enterprises Ltd. Emerging Econ. Cases J. **5**(2), 82–87 (2023). https://doi.org/10.1177/25166042231177212

Matthews, G., et al.: Evolution and revolution: personality research for the coming world of robots, artificial intelligence, and autonomous systems. Personality Individual Differences **169**, 109969 (2021). https://doi.org/10.1016/j.paid.2020.109969

Litwin, A.S., et al.: A forum on emerging technologies. ILR Rev. **75**(4), 807–856 (2022)

# Greening IT Infrastructure: A Focus on Sustainable Cloud Solution

Aarzoo Verma, Sarita Tripathy, Prasant Kumar Pattnaik, and Seema Gupta Bhol(✉)

School of Computer Engineering, KIIT, Bhubaneswar, India
aarzooverma2826@gmail.com, {sarita.tripathyfcs, patnaikprasantfcs,seemaguptabhol.fca}@kiit.ac.in

**Abstract.** The cloud computing has brought a revolution in IT landscape, offering unprecedented accessibility and scalability through virtualized infrastructure. This paper explores the multifaceted aspects of energy utilization in cloud computing, emphasizing server load distribution, job allocation methods, and virtual machine workload management. Moreover, it investigates the potential of green cloud computing to reduce carbon footprints and promote sustainability in the IT sector. Through cost- effectiveness, simplified usability, and reduced energy consumption, cloud computing emerges as a transformative technology with profound environmental implications. By optimizing resource allocation, less energy consuming hardware, and adopting green energy sources, green cloud computing initiatives aim to reduce environmental impact while fulfilling the increasing demand for IT industry. The proposed study focuses on the significance of green cloud computing as a sustainable solution for organizations striving to balance technological innovation with an environmental responsibility.

**Keywords:** Carbon Footprints · SaaS · IaaS · PaaS · Cloud Computing · Green Computing · Load Balancing

## 1 Introduction

The growing adoption of cloud computing across various sectors and businesses has caused a paradigm shift in digital infrastructure, leading in the expansion of data centers hosting a wide range of servers. However, this rapid expansion has brought to the forefront a slew of difficulties, the most prominent of which is the exponential increase in energy use and the resulting rise in carbon emissions. The tremendous heat generated by these processes endangers not just the environment but also human health, emphasizing the critical need for early action and long-term solutions [1]. In response to the pressing environmental and ecological challenges raised by traditional data centre operations, green cloud computing emerges as an appealing and novel solution. Green cloud computing aims to alleviate the negative environmental implications associated with typical cloud infrastructures by implementing cutting-edge solutions focused on power-efficient resource allocation and optimizing energy utilization through smart deployment of IT


R. Kumar et al. (Eds.): ICNGCCA 2025, LNICST 665, pp. 114–123, 2026.
https://doi.org/10.1007/978-3-032-13009-9_10

resources. This forward-thinking strategy, based on the principle of environmental stewardship, attempts to lower operational expenses while also minimizing energy use and carbon emissions. Green cloud computing, inspired by green chemistry concepts, aims to reduce the use of dangerous Chemicals, promote energy-efficient product life cycles, and advocate for responsible recycling of obsolete equipment and manufacturing waste.

The implementation of green cloud computing has the potential to bring a plethora of practical benefits, ranging from a large reduction in energy consumption and improved power efficiency in data centers to a reduced reliance on ecologically harmful equipment. The use of green cloud computing promotes sustainable development and accomplishing long-term environmental sustainability objectives. The basic models (SaaS, IaaS, PaaS) not only underpin the core tenets of cloud computing, but also play an important role in influencing the trajectory of green initiatives, paving the way for a more sustainable and ecologically responsible digital future.

## 2 Literature Review

From last decade, research focus on green computing is continuously increasing. Large number of studies have investigated the various application of green cloud computing and done in-depth evaluations of existing research in this area which are discussed here. Airehrour (2015) highlights the significance of energy efficiency in reducing carbon footprints, emphasizing its critical role in mitigating environmental impact. Furthermore, notable strides in enhancing energy efficiency are recognized, shedding light on the ongoing efforts to address the persistent challenges posed by global energy consumption patterns [2]. S.Thakur (2016) emphasized on assessing carbon usage productivity within the context of cloud architecture, with a particular focus on achieving enhanced energy usages. This entails a thorough examination of how carbon is utilized in the cloud environment, aiming to optimize its productivity while concurrently striving to improve the efficiency of energy consumption practices [3]. F.Shakeel (2017) underscores how cloud computing is growing rapidly and its impact on the proliferation of data centers. It explains how the rise of cloud technology leads to an increase in data center establishments in various locations. By examining the transformation brought about by cloud computing, the paper elucidates why and where data centers are emerging, reshaping their construction and geographical distribution due to the rising demand for cloud services and storage [4]. Sujni Paul (2018) suggests how cloud computing operates, wherein companies utilize extensive server networks to store and share data with customers and other organizations. As more people utilize cloud services, the energy consumed by these servers escalates significantly, resulting in various challenges such as high operational costs. The paper also delves into different facets of cloud computing and the roles users play in the system. It presents the findings of a survey conducted in the UAE and utilizes the Green Cloud Simulator to illustrate the associated impacts [5]. M.Wadhwa (2019) focuses on how green cloud computing offers energy-efficient solutions across different industries. The paper also underscores the importance of managing electric power usages in data hubs to ensure efficient operation without wastage [6]. T.Shree (2020) discusses the release of environmentally harmful gases by cloud computing, emphasizing the necessity for a greener approach. It compares the energy consumption of Google searches with other activities and concludes that the future will witness widespread implementation of green computing in cloud services and its associated benefits [7]. Y.Iano et al. (2021) thoroughly examine the current state of intelligent cloud computing solutions, focusing on factors such as resource utilization and responsiveness. It advocates prioritizing performance and environmental friendliness in future cloud computing advancements. The paper evaluates the efficiency and intelligence of current cloud systems and proposes strategies for further enhancement [8]. Sriram et al. (2022) address various strategies aimed at creating a more environmentally friendly approach to cloud computing by giving importance to renewable energy resources over traditional sources [9]. PA Malla (2023) discusses ways to reduce power consumption in networking for cloud computing. It explains techniques such as creating virtual networks, adjusting resources as needed, and optimizing data traffic. These methods contribute to energy conservation and ensure efficient network operation without excessive power usage [10]. M.Yenugula (2024) explores how cloud computing contributes to sustainable development. Cloud Computing (CC) is seen as a game-changer technology that helps businesses and organizations lessen their environmental footprint. It also opens doors for economic growth and social progress. By leveraging cloud services, companies can reduce their reliance on physical infrastructure, leading to fewer resources used and lower emissions. Additionally, cloud technology enables greater flexibility and efficiency, allowing businesses to adapt more easily to changing demands and markets. Overall, the paper highlights the transformative potential of cloud computing in fostering a more sustainable and prosperous future [11].

## 3 Need of Green Computing Environment

As organizations increasingly recognize the importance of sustainability in their operations, the adoption of green computing practices has emerged as a critical strategy to mitigate the environmental impact of Information Technology (IT) infrastructure. To embark on the journey towards greener computing, it is essential to establish a methodological approach that outlines clear steps and strategies for implementation. This approach provides a structured framework for organizations to initiate and integrate green computing principles into their IT operations effectively. Adaption of green computing strategies in cloud environment increases QoS. The objective is to lessen the burden of carbon emission from IT industry on the planet [12, 13]. Methods for Achieving Green Computing and Improving Energy Economy:

- Data Center Upgrades: Upgrading data centers is essential as older technologies tend to consume more energy and produce excess heat when compared to modern ones.
- Power Management: Implementing power management techniques that involve shutting down and switching off inactive CPUs and other devices after a period of inactivity.

Computers rely on a significant amount of resources housed within their various components, necessitating both raw materials for construction and power for operation. As these devices approach the end of their lifespan, the imperative for recycling becomes increasingly apparent. Therefore, the initial phases of integrating green computing practices entail a comprehensive approach to designing, manufacturing, utilizing,

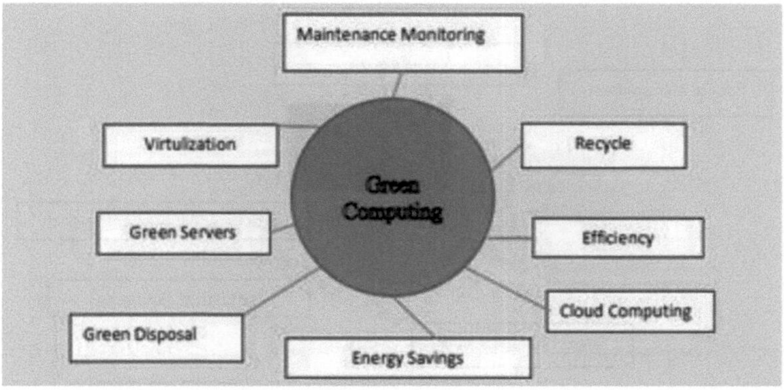


**Fig. 1.** Green Computing

and disposing of products in a manner that minimizes environmental harm. Numerous computer manufacturers and IT companies have demonstrated considerable progress in this endeavor, implementing a variety of measures aimed at reducing the ecological foot-print of computing. These measures encompass adopting designs that consume less energy, sourcing materials that are more environmentally friendly, and establishing recycling programs tailored to handle obsolete hardware. Through these initiatives, the industry is working towards a more sustainable approach to computing, one that acknowledges the importance of resource conservation and environmental responsibility. Green Computing Analysis Eco-friendly cloud solutions present an opportunity for businesses to achieve substantial cost reductions while also conserving energy. Green cloud computing encompasses resource management solutions that streamline resource handling, such as virtualization, simplified resource scheduling, and enhanced monitoring of cloud computing resources [14, 15]. Another key aspect of this approach is the utilization of sustainable resources, prioritizing environmentally conscious practices.

- Heat Reuse: Prolonged use of cloud computing services generates substantial heat, which can be effectively reused with the aid of sustainable resources provided by GCC.
- Sustainable Energy: GCC enables the reuse of energy, including free cooling methods, contributing to sustainable energy practices.

The global expansion of corporations has a considerable environmental influence, notably seen in the rise of infrastructure hubs. These hubs, along with the growing daily travel of employees and the arrival of resources and office materials, compound environmental concerns. Ecofriendly cloud technology emerges as an avenue to diminish environmental impact worldwide, seeking to address these pressing environmental matters [16, 17].

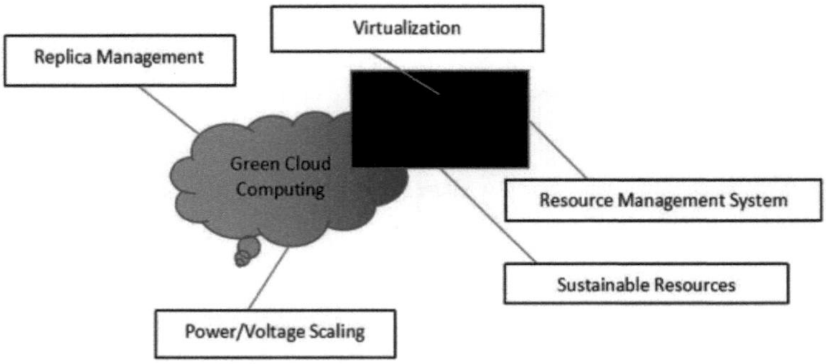


**Fig. 2.** Green Cloud Analysis

## 4 Green Cloud Computing

Green cloud computing encompasses various strategies and initiatives aimed at optimizing resource usage, improving energy efficiency, and mitigating the environmental impact of cloud-based services and infrastructure. A key component of cloud computing are data centers, which house servers used to store and analyse corporate data as well as applications. The computers, cables, cooling systems, networks, and other equipment that make up these data centers consumes more electric power and generates more and more carbon dioxide.One of the primary problems with cloud computing is energy optimization, for which "green cloud computing" was developed as a remedy. Data centre energy consumption has increased due to the growth of data centers and rising power demand by businesses and organizations. Significant energy waste occurs in data centers from underutilized resources and idle servers [18-20].

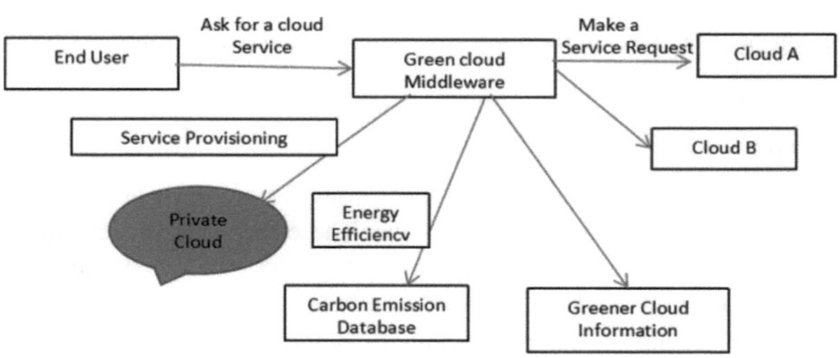


**Fig. 3.** Green Cloud Architecture

Furthermore, the problem of energy wastage due to overloaded servers is addressed through various strategies such as load balancing, virtual machine migration, and job scheduling. These approaches aim to efficiently distribute workloads and optimize resource utilization, ultimately reducing energy waste.

## 5 Load Balancing in Cloud Computing

Load balancing is very important in reducing energy usages and preventing overheating by distributing workloads across multiple servers. This approach is cost-effective and user-friendly, enabling organizations to rapidly develop client applications at a reduced cost. Cloud load balancing offers ease of use for handling website traffic, with effective load balancers managing high-level traffic through network infrastructure and server [21, 22].

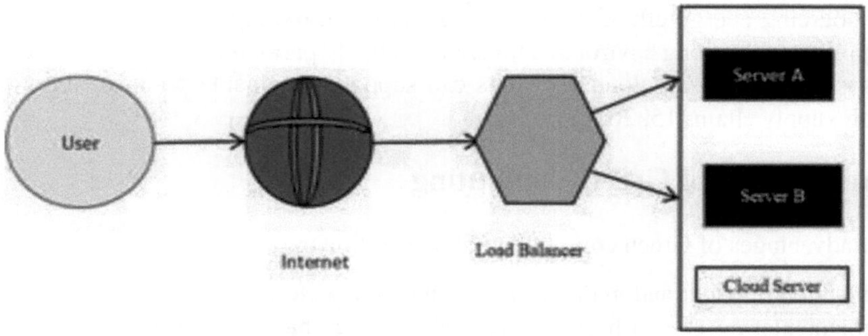


**Fig. 4.** Load Balancing

In the Fig. 4, the user is accessing the system over the internet. The internet traffic is then routed to the load balancer. The load balancer distributes the traffic across the two servers (Server A and Server B). This helps to ensure that the system can handle a high volume of traffic without overloading any one server. Overall, the figure signifies a cloud-based system that is designed to be scalable and reliable. The load balancer helps.

to ensure that the system can handle a high volume of traffic, and the cloud server allows the system to scale up or down as needed.

## 6 Approaches Towards Green Cloud Computing

Green cloud computing represents a transformative strategy for reducing the environmental impact of cloud computing operations while enhancing efficiency and sustainability. Some key approaches include:

- Virtualization: This involves creating virtual instances or environments within physical servers, enabling multiple operating systems and applications to run on a one machine. By distributing total task on less number of servers, virtualization helps in achieving green energy goals.

- Energy-efficient hardware: Especially designed hardware based on the principle of energy efficiency play important role in achieving green energy initiatives [23, 24].
- Dynamic resource allocation: Cloud platforms employ dynamic resource allocation techniques to match computing resources with workload demands in real-time. By scaling resources up or down based on demand, cloud providers can optimize resource utilization and minimize energy waste [25].
- Data center optimization: Data center optimization includes implementing efficient cooling systems, improving airflow management, and utilizing advanced power distribution techniques [6].
- Carbon footprint monitoring and reporting: Cloud providers track and report their carbon emissions and energy usage to stakeholders, enabling transparency and accountability. By monitoring their environmental impact, cloud providers can identify areas for improvement and implement strategies to further reduce their carbon foot-print [7].
- Green procurement practices: Cloud providers can adopt green procurement practices by sourcing energy-efficient hardware, minimizing packaging waste, and selecting suppliers with strong environmental credentials. By partnering with environmentally responsible vendors, cloud providers can support sustainable practices throughout their supply chain [15, 26, 27].

## 7 Advantages of Green Computing

Major advantages of Green computing includes following:

- Reduction of paper and materials usage in the IT sector.
- Implementation of eco-friendly materials such as bamboo and reused plastics in computer manufacturing, minimizing the impact on the ecosystem.
- Energy and cooling cost savings through IT virtualization, allowing multiple computer systems on a single hardware setup and resulting in financial savings.
- Adoption of refurbishment and recycling methods to reduce equipment disposal needs [27].

## 8 Result

Total quantity of greenhouse gases that a corporation, person, car, or other organization emits is referred to as its "carbon footprint." Because of the increased demand that cloud computing creates, its widespread adoption across a variety of industries and companies has resulted in a significant increase in carbon emissions. With each computer consuming 500 kW of energy annually and producing 290 kg of CO2 emissions, cloud computing systems have a major impact on greenhouse gas emissions.

By putting energy-efficient technologies like the quiet PC into practice, carbon emissions can be cut by 40% and green cloud computing can be advanced. Simple actions like maintaining moderate room temperatures can help reduce greenhouse gas emissions, such as CO2 and methane, caused by human activities. The concentration of carbon increases in areas with a higher presence of information technology firms. Figure 5 shows that data center energy consumption is a significant and growing problem for ecological sustainability of planet.

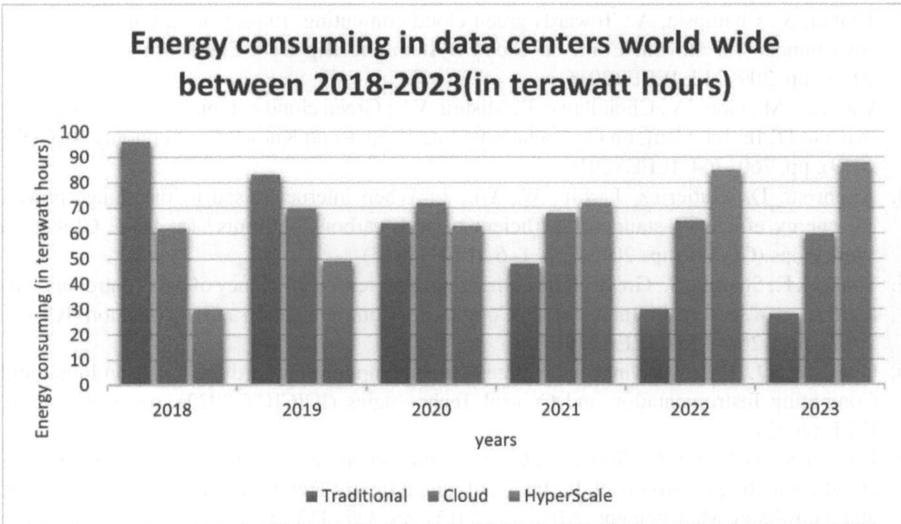


**Fig. 5.** Global Data Centre Energy Consumption from2018 to 2023

## 9 Conclusion and Future Directions

In conclusion, the rapid expansion of the cloud computing industry has brought forth a critical need to address its environmental impact. Recognizing the imperative of economizing and preserving the environment, the concept of Green Cloud Computing (GCC) emerges as a pivotal solution. GCC holds the potential to significantly reduce energy consumption in Internet Data Centres (IDCs) and mitigate the environmental consequences of data centre operations. Furthermore, its role in curbing e-waste.

disposal underscores its immediate relevance in sustainability efforts. By integrating green computing principles with cloud technology, organizations can actively contribute to carbon pollution mitigation and create a more environmentally sustainable work environment. Preserving energy resources for future generations remains paramount, and the integration of GCC becomes fundamental element in the cloud computing technologies. Looking ahead, the future direction of cloud computing will be marked by a steadfast commitment to sustainability and environmental responsibility. Innovations in GCC will drive progress in reducing the carbon footprint of cloud computing operations. Additionally, a focus on life cycle sustainability, regulatory compliance, and continuous research and innovation will shape the evolution of green cloud computing technologies. Embracing these future directions will not only enhance the environmental sustainability of cloud computing but also contribute to building a more resilient and eco-friendly digital ecosystem for generations to come.

## References

1. Sailesh, C., Praneeth, V.S., Koushik, S.S., Sai, V.G.N., Vurukonda, N., Burugari, V.K.: A review on adoption of green cloud computing. In: 7th Int. Conf. on Computing Methodologies and Communication (ICCMC 2023), pp. 1–6. IEEE (2023)

2. Thakur, S., Chaurasia, A.: Towards green cloud computing: impact of carbon footprint on environment. In: 6th Int. Conf. on Cloud System and Big Data Engineering (Confluence 2016), pp. 209–213. IEEE (2016)
3. Wadhwa, M., Goel, A., Choudhury, T., Mishra, V.P.: Green cloud computing—a greener approach to IT. In: Int. Conf. on Computational Intelligence and Knowledge Economy (ICCIKE 2019), pp. 760–764. IEEE (2019)
4. Airehrour, D., Gutierrez, J., Liu, W., Wu, J.: When internet raised to the things power: are energy efficiency standards sufficient to curb carbon footprints? In: IEEE Globecom Workshops (GC Wkshps 2015), pp. 1–6. IEEE (2015)
5. Shakeel, F., Sharma, S.: Green cloud computing: a review on efficiency of data centres and virtualization of servers. In: Int. Conf. on Computing, Communication and Automation (ICCCA 2017), pp. 1264–1267. IEEE (2017)
6. Quraishi, S.J.: Energy savings using green cloud computing. In: 3rd Int. Conf. on Intelligent Computing Instrumentation and Control Technologies (ICICICT 2022), pp. 1496– 1500. IEEE (2022)
7. Patel, Y.S., Mehrotra, N., Soner, S.: Green cloud computing: a review on green IT areas for cloud computing environment. In: Int. Conf. on Futuristic Trends on Computational Analysis and Knowledge Management (ABLAZE 2015), pp. 327–332. IEEE (2015)
8. Shree, T., Kumar, R., Kumar, N.: Green computing in cloud computing. In: 2nd Int. Conf. on Advances in Computing, Communication Control and Networking (ICACCCN 2020),pp. 903–905. IEEE (2020)
9. Yenugula, M., Sahoo, S., Goswami, S.: Cloud computing for sustainable development: an analysis of environmental, economic and social benefits. J. Future Sustainability **4**(1), 59–66 (2024)
10. Londe, V., Math, M.M.: Green computing based cost optimization in cloud computing. In: Int. Conf. on Energy, Communication, Data Analytics and Soft Computing (ICECDS 2017), pp. 37–41. IEEE (2017)
11. More, N.S., Ingle, R.B.: Challenges in green computing for energy saving techniques. In: Int. Conf. on Emerging Trends & Innovation in ICT (ICEI 2017), pp. 73–76. IEEE (2017)
12. Kinkar, K., Bhosale, P., Kasar, A., Gutte, V.: Carbon footprint analysis: need for green cloud computing. In: Int. Conf. on Electronics and Renewable Systems (ICEARS 2022), pp. 1–6. IEEE (2022)
13. Aion, M.K., Bhuiyan, M.N., Jabed, A.: Making the cloud energy efficient: an approach to make the data centers greener. In: Int. Conf. on Informatics, Electronics & Vision (ICIEV 2015), pp. 1–5. IEEE (2015)
14. Rubyga, G., SathiaBhama, P.R.: A survey of computing strategies for green cloud. In: 2nd Int. Conf. on Science Technology Engineering and Management (ICONSTEM 2016), pp. 141–145. IEEE (2016)
15. Jain, A., Mishra, M., Peddoju, S.K., Jain, N.: Energy efficient computing–green cloud computing. In: Int. Conf. on Energy Efficient Technologies for Sustainability (2013), pp. 978–982. IEEE (2013)
16. Kaur, B., Kaur, A.: An Efficient approach for green cloud computing using genetic algorithm. In: 1st Int. Conf. on Next Generation Computing Technologies (NGCT 2015), pp. 10–15. IEEE (2015)
17. Mandal, R., Banerjee, S., Islam, M.B., Chatterjee, P., Biswas, U.: QoS and energy efficiency using green cloud computing. In: Intelligent Internet of Things for Healthcare and Industry, pp. 287–305. Springer, Cham (2022)
18. Sivakumar, N.R.: Investigation study on secured data communication with blockchain and IoT in green cloud computing. In: ICT for Competitive Strategies (ICTCS 2020), pp. 675– 686. Springer, Singapore (2022)

19. Sriram, G.S.: Green cloud computing: an approach towards sustainability. Int. Res. J. Modernization Eng. Technol. Sci. **4**(1), 1263–1268 (2022)
20. Borah, A.D., Muchahary, D., Singh, S.K., Borah, J.: Power saving strategies in green cloud computing systems. Int. J. Grid Distrib. Comput. **8**(1), 299–306 (2015)
21. Bindhu, V., Joe, M.: Green cloud computing solution for operational cost efficiency and environmental impact reduction. J. ISMAC **1**(2), 120–128 (2019)
22. Farooqi, A.M.: Comparative Analysis of Green Cloud Computing. Int. J. Adv. Res. Comput. Sci. **8**(2) (2017)
23. Pandya, S.S.: Green Cloud Computing. Int. J. Inf. Comput. Technol. (2014)
24. Marashi, A.: Improving Data Center Power Consumption & Energy Efficiency. VXCHNGE (2020)
25. Ohri, A.: Green Cloud Computing: A Beginner's Guide. Jigsaw Academy (2020)
26. Breckling, J.: The Analysis of Directional Time Series: Applications to Wind Speed and Direction, vol. 61. Springer, Heidelberg (2012)
27. Thillaiarasu, N., ChenthurPandian, S.: RETRACTED ARTICLE: a novel scheme for safeguarding confidentiality in public clouds for service users of cloud computing. Cluster Comput. **22**(Suppl. 1), 1179–1188 (2019)

# Author Index





R. Kumar et al. (Eds.): ICNGCCA 2025, LNICST 665, p. 125, 2026.
https://doi.org/10.1007/978-3-032-13009-9

MIX
Papier aus verantwortungsvollen Quellen
Paper from responsible sources
FSC® C105338

If you have any concerns about our products,
you can contact us on
**ProductSafety@springernature.com**

In case Publisher is established outside the EU,
the EU authorized representative is:
**Springer Nature Customer Service Center GmbH**
**Europaplatz 3, 69115 Heidelberg, Germany**

Printed by Libri Plureos GmbH
in Hamburg, Germany